Words

A JOURNEY TO THE LIGHT WITHIN

By

DARLENE VERSAK

Published By Tierra Destiny Reid
& TDR Brands Publishing

Copyright © 2022 Darlene Versak

All rights reserved. This book is copyright material and must not be copied, reproduced, transferred, distributed, leased, licensed or used in any way except as specifically permitted in writing by the author, as allowed under the terms and conditions under which it was purchased or as strictly permitted by applicable copyright law. Respective authors own all copyrights not held by the publisher. In no way is it legal to reproduce, duplicate, or transmit any part of this document in either electronic means or printed format.

Any unauthorised distribution or use of this text may be a direct infringement of the Author's rights, and those responsible may be liable in law accordingly.

ISBN: 978-1-947574-64-9

Published By: Published By Tierra Destiny Reid & TDR Brands Publishing

Acknowledgements

The Way of Mastery; pages 43-44: "Who am I? I am the extension of Love in form. I have never been born and I will never taste death. I am infinite and eternal. I shine forth as a sunbeam to the sun. I am the effect of God's Love. And I stand before you to love you."

Thank you to friends and family – you know who you are. You have supported, encouraged, questioned and opened me up to see how Love shows up in this world. Buddha said, "When the student is ready, the teacher will appear." This is how I feel about Jen Halterman. Following the breadcrumbs led me to her and my own freedom. I am appreciative and grateful for her Life Coaching, guidance and friendship.

Shout out to the Bad Ass Ladies – a group she created to learn about visibility, which turned into sharing awareness and vulnerability and now we're simply friends. I've met and studied with two other teachers (who also made a huge impact) Varian Brandon and Alison Crow. Both coaches speak the truth – even when it's uncomfortable. Both leaders' model what it means to evolve consciousness and run their own business. No, we're not regular. Several books that were key for my evolution are The Bible, A Course In Miracles (ACIM), The Way of Mastery and The Gene Keys. Each book explores Love in all it's expressions and for that, I am grateful.

A special thank you to Michelle Perron who did the initial editing of the book. Her thoughtful comments, her wonderful way with punctuation, her time and enthusiasm for this project are most appreciated. I'd also like to thank Tierra Destiny and Legacy Publications for helping me with the formatting and publishing of this experience. Sometimes the words poured through me. Thank you Love for allowing me to be a channel for your words.

Dedication

I dedicate this book to Gloria. She was my playmate, friend and mother. The first person I truly loved.

Table of Contents

Foreword	7
Wake Up	16
Cancer – 15 Years Ago	17
Facing Hard Truths And Surviving (a few years later)	18
Fear, Dying and Choice	22
An Intimate Experience	30
Love Or Fear	36
The Beginning (57 Years Ago)	40
My Childhood	46
Gloria's Story	52
Death – What I Was Taught – Peering Through	54
My Lens For Death	54
Adult Version of Death – Wiping The Lens	55
Forgiveness	62
Redemption	66
The Flicker of Discontent	70
The 3:00 am Call From My Soul To Wake The Fuck Up	71
The Song on The Radio	74
Finally, I Choose Me	80
Alfie	82
What I Learned From Grief	84
Equality	90
I Am as God Created Me (Lesson 94, 162, 176) – A Course in Miracles (ACIM)	92
Writing My Sage	96
If You Want to Change The World, It Starts With Yourself	98
What God Have You Made?	100
Romantic Love	104
Again And Again – A Fable For This time	105
The Invitation	108
The Power of One Step	112
The Call	118
What we focus on grows	122
All We Have is Now	124
I am Not A Victim. I am A Creator.	125
Resources	130

Foreword

This is a story of awakening. A choice made to listen to the whispers of soul and walk a path less traveled. Every life is filled with pain and suffering to some degree. Every life has joy and happiness as well. We live. We fall in love. People arrive. People leave. We experience kindness and compassion. There is betrayal and disappointment. We die. The words we use to describe what happens during our journey are important. The story we tell ourselves and the world matters. The words we use will create the next story and the next story, which will validate the first story. Our words cast spells. We can be unconsciously creating or consciously creating. The choice is ours. Make no mistake - we are always creating our life. We do it with thoughts, words, and feelings which, full of vibrational energy, spur us to action or inaction. The beautiful thing is? We get to decide. We are in charge. Despite what anyone has ever told you, it is your life. You can choose why, what and how you'll live it.

I invite you to walk along the path with me. Imagine we are holding hands and walking together. Enclosed are vignettes in time. Snapshots of moments captured in words. I share some of what I've walked through. I've dated some of the poems so you can see how my perspective changed over time with my choice to return to Love. All of the pieces were written over the span of seven years, and my perspective has changed from the beginning writings to now. I did not "fix" the judgments I wrote about. I've tried to capture what awakening looks, feels and sounds like, although it's impossible to truly know another's evolution. Everyone evolves differently and that is how it is. There are some basic truths we all encounter along the way. How we choose to embody those truths, well, that's what makes us unique.

I have a good friend, Randy, who told me he has known three distinct versions of me: one in my 20s (Hey, party girl); the second in my 30s and 40s (a married-mom-religious woman), and the third who I am today (sacred rebel of kindness, a devotee to Truth and Love who likes to wander in nature and love on people).

He told me he likes this version best. So do I.

Join me as we wander in words.

Words

A JOURNEY TO THE LIGHT WITHIN

Dear Reader,

Thank you for purchasing and reading this book. I appreciate you. This book is a little different than most, in that, it's been created to be interactive. I've included song links to YouTube which you can copy and paste if you're reading on Kindle or you can access by searching YouTube or by typing in the link directly. As these song links come up, I invite you to listen to the songs in their entirety, prior to moving to the next page. Perhaps, you'll play the song as you continue to the next page. You may not want to listen to the songs. Each choice is okay. There is no right or wrong way to wander in these words.

Pictures add a visual component to the stories and poems add texture. The request is to drink them in as they arise and feel what you feel.

You'll also find the infinity symbol:

∞

When you see this symbol, it's an invitation to stop, pause and contemplate or meditate for a few minutes. Close your eyes, relax and go within. Breathe, be mindful of your breath for 2-3 minutes. You can make it more or less. You can do whatever feels right for you.

The book is meant to be an experience. It's my experience of transforming my mindset. It chronicles, from different angles, my return to the Light within. Wherever you are in your journey, know that you are not alone. We are all in this together. You are a precious child of the Universe.

I love you!

Darlene

Antelope Canyon June 2017
"Words" (Live in Las Vegas, 1997-One Night Only) – Bee Gees
https://www.youtube.com/watch?v=pkqwRC23HN8

WISDOMS WHISPERS

Whisper wisdom
Help me please
Find a way
Make sense of it all
Guidance
Messages
Hidden
Gems
To be found
Eyes open
Hands unclenched
Heart gaping
Speak to me please
I'm ready
Deep inhale
Huge exhale
Again
And again

DAV 9-7-17

Words

Words are symbols used to communicate the meaning of something. Words stand on a page or hang in the air, representing something else. They are what we use to convey meaning to each other. Words are, at best, once removed from what they are describing. Words are magical. They contain energy to create our wildest dreams and our worst nightmares. The words we use to describe our lives are powerful. What we think brings color to our perception. We can be awesome or we can be shit. The energy in the words we use determines whether we live in heaven or hell, no matter what is happening externally around us.

Sometimes words can complicate. The meaning that we've applied to a word may be different from the way someone else understands it. We learn as we grow up what different words mean and what we learn may or may not be true, depending on our lens. The words I've gathered in this book are an examination of how words can be used to illuminate a subject (love) or create illusions (fear). We are part nature (what we arrive here with, our talents, innate skills and abilities, our inclinations) and nurture (what we were taught by our families, schools, culture of our time, nations, etc.). It is the nurture part, the programming we pick up throughout life about how to socialize and how to be loved in this world, that I'd like us to look at, play with, contemplate and ultimately be aware of so that we can live at choice and create our lives.

Awareness is the key that opens the lock to the prison I put myself in. The prison I built to protect me. A prison I built to blame others and put them in cells in my mind so we are both held captive. Them the judged and me the jailor. When I become aware of the programming I've been taught, I get to look at it from the vantage point of, "Is this true for me? Is this really true?" When I do the work to examine my life, to examine my whys and unravel the different stories that have been running quietly in the background, only then can I be free. Then I can be at choice. Waking up is like an Alice in Wonderland adventure: you never know when the white rabbit is going to pop up and scare you. I can guarantee you that if you make the decision to wake up, if you choose to think for yourself, to live in allowance (break up with judgment) and be who you be - you will be free. The shame, blame game will be over. You'll be in charge of whether you want to jump on the drama triangle or not. It can be easy or it can be complicated – you get to choose. We are presented with so many choices. Life really is a pick-your-own-adventure book. What will I choose today?

There is my business, your business and divine business. Transformation is my business. It's where I learn to be steward of myself. The words written here are inspired by events in my life. This is my journey down the rabbit hole. Grab a cup of tea (or coffee with turmeric, black pepper and cream) and enjoy!

SYMBOLS

Words stand as symbols
Providing elucidation or confusion
in my mind
Combing files from the past
finding
ideas and associations
Events and happenings
To give meaning
And context
To
Now

Darlene Versak 9/22/20

Wake Up

I am a divine expression having a human experience.

Close your eyes and repeat that sentence. Contemplate the idea for a moment.

We are energy having a human experience. The physical, emotional, mental and spiritual parts of us are the four layers that make up each human being. How these layers work together determines if we are in flow. Our physical body will tell us when something is wrong. It sends us messages all the time. However, it's up to us to listen and pay attention to or ignore the warning signals. Choice, as my friend and Life Coach Jen Halterman says, is my superpower. Always! If we ignore our body, it will come back to bite us. In the end, it always does.

Cancer – 15 Years Ago

I felt the lump in my right breast. It was small, but hard, and I knew it wasn't good. Of course, I hoped it would go away. I hoped it would disappear like my monthly cycle - maybe they were connected and it was just hormones all bunched up in my breast tissue. But no, it didn't go away, and it took a week or two of mental debate with myself to call the doctor and make the appointment. The mammogram was ordered and the diagnosis was a cyst (thank God). The doctor would drain it and that would be the end of it. Phew! Once it was drained, I figured it was over. I was wrong. They couldn't drain it in the office because the needle would not penetrate the cyst. Instead, the doctor decided that it would need to be taken out surgically and biopsied.

After the procedure, the doctor called me into his office to talk to him. If that has ever happened to you, you will understand that a doctor wanting to see you in person and to talk to you is never good. I went to his office and he told me that the cyst was benign. However, they found cells surrounding it that indicated I had a 70% greater chance of developing breast cancer than the general population a condition called LCIS, an acronym for Lobular Carcinoma In-Situ. The doctor had awful bedside manner. He talked to me like he was reading from a script: no emotion, just the facts Ma'am. He was the Dragnet of doctors (a reference to a cop drama from the 1960s - Google that shit if you're younger than 50 or don't watch Hulu). At this point, I had nothing. I had "a greater chance" of developing something. I was given my options – mastectomy, tamoxifen for five years (take a drug that may cause other stuff and may prevent cancer from developing … or not), or monitor the situation (aka do nothing but see the doctor more often and have more mammograms). I chose the last option. At this point, I had nothing but a red flag.

Facing Hard Truths And Surviving (a few years later)

Nobody, and I mean nobody, desires to receive a diagnosis of cancer. Depending on the type and stage when it's found, it could be a death sentence. Shit gets real when the doctor calls you and says the diagnosis is LCIS. The name I'll never forget. For those of you unfamiliar with the medical term, LCIS is a form of breast cancer (carcinoma is the blinking red flag term for cancer). When you get a call from a doctor (red flag #1) and he tells you he has some bad news (red flag #2), asks if you're not driving and in a place that you can talk (red flag #3), you know it's not gonna be good. Cancer is not a word for the faint of heart. He was talking, but my ego was shouting louder, moving into damage control mode. Freaking out in fear, the question being "Am I going to die?" Here's the reality: we're all going to die. We just don't know when. Up to this point, my ego had done a pretty good job of keeping that thought out of my reality. Sure, I was going to die, but it would be a long, long ways away. I think that's how we live with the fact that we're all dying - we tuck it away in a soft blanket of denial. If we deny the fact that our bodies die, then we never really have to choose to live. At least, not today anyway.

I'd been getting six-month mammograms for a couple of years and they'd all gone well. This time there was something developing - a cluster of cells. A decision would need to be made. The roulette ball of cancer landed on my spot.

Stunned and in shock, I hung up the phone. I would be scheduling more appointments, getting second opinions, and traveling a road that I had not been down before. My sons were 12 and 10 at the time. I did not want to leave them yet. I wanted them to grow up with a mom.

Cancer is a statistics game. It's all about the odds. It's like gambling with your life based on what treatment you pick. I spoke to another surgeon. "Yup, you've got it." I spoke to a plastic surgeon about having a mastectomy. He showed me pictures. They were frightening and plain awful pictures of women who survived, but they were disfigured. Oh my God, this can't be happening. Denial kicks in as necessary when we're overwhelmed. I wanted someone to tell me what to do. No one would. No one would say, "This is what you should do." They would present the facts, give me survival numbers, statistics to back up choices … yet no one would tell me what I should do. At the end of the day, the decision was mine when it came down to choosing amongst the treatment options. I would have to live with whatever choice I made. That was the bottom line.

I had only one doctor left to see. She was a radiation oncologist at Jefferson Hospital in Philadelphia, PA. She was highly recommended. If I chose surgery and I needed radiation afterwards, her job would be to inform me of what that would look like and present more statistics based on my choices. I knew this was the last doctor I would see prior to making a decision. I felt lost, rudderless, without direction. The night before my appointment, I dropped to my knees beside my bed and prayed for someone to please tell me what to do. Please God send me an angel. I needed an answer fast, and so far, I wasn't certain what to do. I was leaning toward the mastectomy, because numbers-wise, that made sense. However, what was the best decision for me?

Honestly, I don't remember the doctor's name. My brain has fuzzed out some of the details of the encounter. She was a woman in her 40s. What I remember about that appointment, about that day, is that she took time with me. She asked me for my story. It was long. I'd gone to a breast doctor because I'd had a lump. He palpitated it and announced it was a cyst. He took a syringe to drain it, couldn't, biopsied it and sent the cyst to the lab. The results came back, there were marker cells that pointed to the fact that I had a 70% greater chance of developing breast cancer. Now, I have it. What did I want to do? Three choices: 1. Mastectomy; 2. Take tamoxifen (which had all kinds of side effects); or 3) Do nothing but watch and wait. I decided to do nothing, as nothing was wrong. Why poke the bear? Let's just see if anything develops. This meant I had to get a mammogram every six months. I also decided to find a new breast surgeon ('cause the first one had shit for people skills).

New surgeon found, visited and a baseline was put in place. It was several years later when the cells began to grow and I had something forming in my right breast. In the fall of 2006, the bad mammogram arrived, I was diagnosed with LCIS. Here I am faced with new choices: 1) Mastectomy; 2) Remove the area in question and hope there were no more "bad" cells around it (see, if they take it out and it doesn't have clear margins around it, they have to go back in and take more out, or just do the mastectomy); or do nothing. Yes, do nothing was still a choice. Hence, this is why I am here.

She asked me, "What do you want?"

"Excuse me, what?" I replied.

"What do you want to happen?" she queried.

"I want to see my kids grow up. I want them to have a mom throughout their childhood and teenage years. I want them to know they are loved unconditionally," I responded.

She listened intently as I spoke. Then, silence.

"Would you like to know what I would do?" she asked.

"Yes, please!" I implored. Finally, a doctor who was going to tell me what they would do if faced with a similar situation.

"If you want to live, with the best chances, I would get the mastectomy and here is why…" And on she went, explaining statistically why it made the most sense. I don't think I really heard anymore. My husband at the time had to work that day. He was great about coming to all my appointments; however, I was alone on this one. In that moment, I realized that my prayer had been answered. Someone just told me what to do, and it matched what I was thinking. My decision was made. My soul and heart had been leaning this way; however, the three surgeries that were part of the deal were daunting to contemplate and I knew I was at a crossroads. Did I want to live or not? Making this choice gave me the best odds for survival. There was much to face moving forward. As she continued to speak, I thought, This is what an angel looks like." I knew my angel in flesh had arrived and helped me, as I had asked.

LESSON I LEARNED FROM THE DECISION

Inside each of us, there is a still place of knowing that exists. The wisdom that exists in this place can only be heard in silence, in between the gaps of thoughts. Wisdom lives in the pause. I was leaning toward the choice of having a mastectomy because this is what that inner place was gently telling me to do. However, at that time I didn't trust myself. I wasn't sure I had the knowledge necessary to firmly stand behind that decision. I decided to choose differently from how I had in the past. I chose to go inward and ask the Universe for guidance. The Bible taught me "Ask and you shall receive." "Seek and you shall find." The Universe is always conspiring to give you exactly what you ask for. This is why words can either be uplifting and create wonderful situations or they can attract to us exactly what we want to avoid. Our words are powerful.

In this instance, I asked the Universe for guidance; an answer to the question of what I should do to treat the LCIS diagnosis. Thankfully, the next day, a doctor told me exactly what she would do if it were her. I've talked to doctors after this situation and all of them said they would never tell a patient what to do, mostly for liability reasons. However, I am forever grateful for this woman, who spoke to me as one human to another. My angel with a stethoscope gave me the courage to make my decision, and for that I am grateful.

Fear, Dying and Choice

The surgery was complete. I opened my eyes to see my husband at the time, standing over me. I felt groggy from the anesthesia and was unable to keep my eyes open for long. I asked, "Is it over?"

"Yes," he replied, "It went well." He smiled. All I could feel in that moment was pain - and it was excruciating. I moaned. The nurse handed me the toggle switch to a morphine drip. She told me to push the button anytime I felt pain. I felt pain, so I pushed the button. A warm rush of a drug sped through my veins but in a few minutes, the relief was gone. The pain returned. I pushed the button again, nothing. I kept pushing it, over and over. She saw what I was doing and touched my left arm "Dear, it only works every 15 minutes." In that moment, I was living to push that button. The thought came to me - this is what agony feels like.

I laid there in limbo praying for the pain to end.

My eyes fluttered open later to see my doctor. "Everything went well. We got it all. Everything slided right out. You are going to be fine." I thought it odd at the time that he used the word "slided." But I guess if you're a surgeon dealing in cancer, they really don't know what they're going to find until they open you up. I think there can be things growing in places not seen in films. There can be tendrils extending behind and out, connecting/attached to different organs. Cancer spreads insidiously. The visual provided by the word "slided" assured me that there were no attachments. He sliced open my boob and slid the fatty tissue out.

He then handed the operation over to the plastic surgeon, who put the expanders in and sewed me back up. Well, it didn't all go perfectly. The plastic surgeon informed me later that when he put the right implant in, he must have nicked it with the scalpel. So, he had to undo his beautiful work of sewing me back up, take the deflated expander out, put a new one in and sew me back up. My right side would have a deeper scar. He didn't say that. It just does, and I understand why. The left side hardly has a scar. The right is unmistakable. I imagine it, too, would have looked good had it not been necessary for him to rip out the seam and then resew it again. I made a story about that in my head. I imagine he was tired sewing it up the second time around. I understand. I've sewn things before and when you rip the seam and try to piece it back together, it's difficult. It's hard to have it look smooth with the least amount of puckering.

I started to watch the clock in and out of consciousness to try to gauge when I could hit that button again. I was flat on my back and down for the count. At some point, they took the morphine drip away and I was put on some other pain med via IV. They were weaning me off the best pain meds, getting my body used to its new reality. It was the beginning process of allowing the body to heal.

I don't sleep in a hospital. There is too much going on in the hallways. Sounds of machines measuring respiration and vital signs fill the room. Being attached to an IV stuck in your arm limits your mobility. It's all so uncomfortable. I found myself awake in the deep night between the hours of 2-5 AM. You know it's not natural for you to be awake at that time. However, when you're in pain to any degree, relaxing and sleeping is damn near impossible. You consciously know that, when you sleep, you allow your body to heal. Yet, pain is a great barrier to relaxation, which is what allows you to fall asleep. Eventually, exhaustion kicks in and you float in between sleep and awake.

The dark night of my soul came at 4 AM. I was in agony. I wanted to die. The morphine was long gone and the lighter pain meds seemed to be a joke. The pain was excruciating and overwhelming. In tears, I asked God to please end this and take me. I was choosing out. I was done.

At that precise moment, I heard a voice, clear and distinct. "Get up." I stopped crying on a dime and looked around the room. What? What did you say? "Get up and walk." In terms of this world, I can't explain that voice. Some may say it was my ego, a hallucination or vestiges of the pain meds. However, I believe the voice I heard was my soul voice. It was clear, calm and commanding. "Get up and walk." WTF - who's that? And then again. I knew to listen. I can't tell you why, I just did. I pressed the nurse call button. They don't come in when you push the call button in the middle of the night. They want to make sure before they get up that they need to come in. The intercom came on: "Can I help you?"

I asked, "Can I walk?" The nurse got so excited. "Yes! Do you want to walk now?"

"Yes," I responded. "That's awesome," she said, "I'll be right in."

She arrived in the room and I said "I wasn't sure if I could get up." She said the plan was to get me moving in the morning. "Moving helps the body to heal quicker - the sooner you get moving, the quicker you will heal," she announced. She seemed genuinely excited. I guess not many people ask the night after their surgery to get up and walk.

She was happy and super enthusiastic that I was ready to start walking early. The nurses attached me to a movable IV pole and detached the other monitors. I stood up for the first time in almost 24 hours. Still a little wobbly I held onto the IV pole. "OK," the nurse said, "Take a few steps and see how you feel." Slowly, I began to walk with the nurse by my side. My first few steps were gentle and I realized that the world did not end. The nurse's station was right outside my room, which was in the corner of the hallway. I was about halfway down the hallway from my room when I told her I was OK. I wanted to walk alone and I hoped that if I told her I was OK she'd let me walk alone. I told her I didn't need her assistance. It was going to take me some time, but I was able to walk by myself. Albeit slowly, but I was doing it. I told her, "My plan is to go to the end of the hall and then back to the room." She eyed me over, considering whether she should trust me, and tentatively went to the nurses' station, watching me as I walked. When I reached the end of the hallway, I turned around. I gave her the thumbs up and she ducked behind the nurse's station. I started the long walk back to the room. I'm not gonna lie, it was painful. But I was moving.

After surgery, the last thing I wanted to do was move. The pain was paralyzing. I thought that if I sat still and curled up into a ball, it would be better. The irony is when you start your body moving, when you get your energy moving, THAT is when you start to heal. It's counterintuitive, but being that we are energy, that is how our body heals. Yes, we need rest, but we also need to move, hence the reason why rehab is prescribed after most surgeries. We move our bodies back to health. The body knows how to heal itself. When we have a cut, we don't stare at it and tell it what to do. The body's immune system rallies and surrounds the affected area and heals it without us doing anything. Well, sometimes we'll add antibiotic ointment and/or a Band-Aid to keep dirt and infection from taking hold. However, for the most part, the body knows what to do.

By the time I returned to my hospital room, I was still in pain; however, the pain was no longer overwhelming. I was more exhausted. They put me back in bed and I slept until morning. The feelings of wanting to die had passed. The pain was still there, but I knew it wasn't forever. I would heal. I would get better, eventually.

What did I have to surrender to get the gift that pain is temporary? Pain has a message to give you if you can sit in it. If you can feel it and ask, "What is this pain telling me?" No, we shouldn't inflict it on ourselves although we do at times. We all experience pain. It's inevitable in the human condition. We feel physical, emotional, mental and spiritual pain at different times in our lives. It's what we do with that pain that matters. We can use awareness to clear the pain. I have a pain in my leg, go to the doctor, he x-rays it and I have a broken bone. It's set. It heals and we clear that pain. The person we thought was the love of our lives betrays us. We leave and feel pain in our heart. In time, we look at the relationship, apply the awareness that forgiveness is required for us to heal. Hopefully, we learn from it and move on. Problems arise when we avoid pain. We avoid separation. We avoid confrontation. No one likes the pain of disconnection, whether it's pain in the body, the head, the heart or the soul. Pain is our body's way of telling us something has happened. Something is wrong. Move. Pivot. Change what you're doing, etc. Pain is a messenger, a wakeup call.

My perception of the voice in my hospital room the night of my surgery is that I had an encounter with my higher self, or God, who commanded my whining, complaining victim self awake. Almost like a slap to the face of a person who is hysterical. Hearing something out of this world literally woke me up in that moment to get to the business of healing. At least that's my perspective of what happened.

THE STRUGGLE WITH PAIN

Let's talk about physical pain first. Sometimes pain is temporary, meaning we know logically that it won't last. For example, when you skin your knee. The pain is intense at first, subsides a bit as a scab is formed, and then aches the next day or two as your body begins to heal. Then it subsides, maybe starts to itch a bit as the skins heals over, and perhaps a scar is left to mark the spot that skin has been broken. Sometimes pain is long-term. Nerves in a back flair up and send pain messages to the brain. Drugs can be taken, massage, chiropractor, acupuncture but nothing seems to ease the relentless message of pain to the brain. When we are in pain, all we desire is for the pain to stop. Pain in all of its various forms (physical, emotional, mental and spiritual) is something we attempt to avoid.

Mental, emotional and spiritual pain are similar. Avoidance is the word of the day. The challenge to be aware of is that if you live, you will experience pain. In the world of time, loss is inevitable. From a spiritual perspective, you never experience loss, because this is life school. We are in a movie titled "Your Life." In this world, everyone's body will die. That's a fact. Everyone that we know will die. No one wants to talk about, let alone think about it. It's true. Even to think about that brings pain and distress to most minds. However, what's also true is that everything that exists in this world is a form of energy and energy does not die. It changes form. We are a spark of divine light inhabiting a human body for whatever time we're here, and then we go back to the light, which means it is impossible for us to die. Yes, our human bodies die; however, our souls, our essence continues on.

So why is there pain? Pain is also a teacher. We learn from pain. Sometimes we learn what not to do. For instance, don't touch the fire. Once you've been burned, you remember the pain of being burned and will avoid that happening again. We take our past experience of pain and apply that to navigating our way through the world.

Sometimes, though, we avoid living in order to avoid pain - and that was never the intention. Gabor Mate, a physician in Canada who treats addiction, suggests that when dealing with addicts, the question shouldn't be, "Why the addiction?" The question should be, "Why the pain? What pain or trauma did you experience that now has you turning to a substance or behavior to take the pain away?" The addiction is the symptom. The pain is the cause. If we can get to the root of it, allow it to come up, apply love to it, then maybe we can heal the person.

Love is the most courageous thing you will do in this world. It is the only thing of value in an illusionary world. What do I mean? Love is the only thing that endures forever. When we truly love someone, even if we are not with them, that love…it doesn't die. Unconditional love is just that – it has no conditions to be necessary. I love you. Period. I love you is a complete sentence. Now, I may not like your behavior and choose not to be with you, but if I'm honest, I still love you.

∞

Bryce Canyon June 2017

https://www.youtube.com/watch?v=QUQsqBqxoR4

"Brave" (Official Video) – Sara Bareilles

DANCING AND SCARS

Words
Spoken
Written
Thought
become
breadcrumbs
appearing
on a trail
Go this way
Turn right
Simple steps
Dancing in time
Leading to
Stories of tragedy
And triumph
Love lost
and found

I trace
In memory
Crooked Lines
of pain
Sweet scars
Once
Tender to touch
Now
Fading
Into forgiveness
What
Have I learned

You are brave
Wake up
Beautiful dreamer
Follow the
Magical trail
One crumb
At a time
Awaken to peace
And be
Who you were
created to be
Love

D. Versak 11/27/19

An Intimate Experience

I'd always been the one to help others. That's why this was so hard. I hesitated. Becky, one of my close friends, asked again: "What can I do for you?"

Seconds that felt like agony passed; I struggled with the question. How do you ask someone for what you really need? How should I phrase it? Should I ask? It was so foreign to me. Sensing and feeling what everyone else needed was my forte.

Becky continued, "Do you need me to make dinner?"

"No," I replied. "I actually have a grid set up for the next two weeks with the names of neighbors, friends and family who are bringing us dinner." I answered slowly.

Becky would not relent.

"Do you need me to clean the house for you?"

"No, Doreen is coming to clean tomorrow afternoon," I replied with a waver in my voice.

She hesitated. It had suddenly become more important than anything, yet it was such a simple thing really.

"There is something you could do for me. I mean if you have a little time and if it's not too much to ask," I asked as my voice quivered ever so slightly with emotion.

"Sure, whatever it is, I'll do it!" Becky replied enthusiastically sensing the importance of what was to be asked of her.

"Do you think you could come over and wash my hair?" I blurted out, holding my breath for the response.

"Absolutely! When is good?" she replied with a slight uneasiness in her voice.

"Tomorrow morning around 9 AM … will that work for you?" I held my breath and felt stupid for how hard it was to ask.

"Yup, that's fine. I'll see you then!" Becky excitedly replied.

"OK, see you then," I answered.

My arms were basically immobilized as a result of the surgery. I wasn't allowed to, nor could I, raise my arms above my head. I'd managed to wash my body, but the now oily hair was a logistics and vanity problem. If you can't raise your arms, you can't wash your hair. I hadn't allowed anyone to come and see me in the hospital. My gatekeeper held them at bay. But all the people that I'd helped over the years and people who cared about me would be arriving at my front step shortly, and my pride forced me to ask for help in the end.

I planned ahead in my mind how this would work. However, I had no idea that the act itself would bring me emotionally to my knees.

The next morning, always prepared, I brought the shampoo and towel downstairs. The brush and red Norelco hair dryer were brought down with the second trip and TRESemme hair spray just in case there was something to actually capture and hold in place at the end. I wished the gatekeeper could/would wash my hair. I thought he would rush. His hands would be clumsy. He seemed unaware of how to handle me gently. I knew it would be better for a woman to wash and blow dry my hair.

Becky arrived looking nervous, too. I could see the fear of what I looked like in her eyes. I gulped at her mirror eyes.

"OK, we have to do this at the kitchen sink so I can bend over, and you'll have enough room to do your thing," I tentatively explained.

"Sure, wherever you want," Becky answered quickly. It was clear she was wading in uncharted territory. Usually when someone had surgery, you dropped off dinner or a banana bread. Who asked you to wash their hair? Thank God she was game to help.

I leaned over the sink and Becky turned the water on. She felt it to make sure it wasn't too hot. Lukewarm. She smiled…perfect! The refreshing stream of water trickled over my head and I thought this must be what it feels like to a baby when it's baptized. Becky put the shampoo in the palm of her hand and slowly, and ever so gently, massaged it into my scalp. The smell of flowers filled my senses. I closed my eyes. It felt so good for someone, anyone, to play with my hair. I was standing so close to Becky while she worked in the lather that I was breathing in the cotton top she was wearing as her arms and hands circled my head. It wasn't a sexual moment - it was an intimate moment. One soul stood directly next to another soul. That's what this was. I was utterly vulnerable and at the mercy and love of another human being, and this person did not disappoint. As the shampoo was being rinsed from my head, tears joined the bubbles down the drain. I was humbled. Becky put the towel around my head, with tears in her eyes, and she hugged me ever so gently and said, "It's OK, it's going to be OK."

LESSON LEARNED

The gift that goes both ways is receiving. Both people in the exchange receive something. The giver watches with delight as they let go of something to another. They feel the energy of letting go in love. The receiver feels the energy of love, freely given to them. When we are giving with no strings attached, and when we receive the same, it is a holy thing. Sacred. It is love swimming between two souls and it's an exchange of energy at the highest vibration. I learned that I cannot only be a giver. I had some learning to do about allowing others to give to me. Allowing Becky to give to me, I, in turn, was learning about how to receive.

Blue Lake Trail (Northern Cascades) Washington State June 2019
https://www.youtube.com/watch?v=oXqPjx94YMg
"Constant Craving" – k.d. Lang

HUNGER

I'm hungry for
I don't know what
I crave
This
That
The other

The space
Inside
Between
Around
Each word
Thought
Feeling
An empty
Hole
Impatiently
Wanting
To be filled
A Square Piece
Never quite
fits

It hadn't
Occurred
to me
That the
Answer
Might be
in breath
This one
The next
And so on
Remember
Who you are

Darlene Versak 4-29-20

Love Or Fear

The world as we knew it ended. COVID-19 seemingly came from nowhere. A highly contagious virus that spread across and around the globe exponentially. It is a historic event. A defining point in history that affected everyone in this world. History will be written about the actions occurring in the present time. For the United States, 9/11 would be the closest point of previous history for comparison. The world would change in unimaginable ways as a result of germs that sickened, and in some cases killed, people. History is written by the survivors and the people in power. What will be said about us? Who are we? What will emerge to define this generation of human beings who faced an unseen enemy that could be anywhere (in people, on surfaces) that took some and left others? No one would be left unscathed. Suffering occurred physically for some and mentally for others; however, this event is affecting everyone. In a very short amount of time, our economy and how people make money has been upended. How people live their lives will be changed from this time forward.

Grocery stores, pharmacies and life-sustaining businesses are the allowed economy now. We are living in a pandemic. A pandemic is defined as "a disease prevalent over a whole country or world." We have been asked to stay home to avoid the spread of the virus. "Social distancing" (staying six feet away from other humans and avoiding contact) is the catch phrase of the day. Although, in reality, it is physical distancing. We share eye contact and smiles from beneath masks. Maybe a few words if we choose to, but that is all. "Wash your hands" is today's mantra.

We face the biggest decision of our lives. What do we believe? Love or fear? Whatever the choice as creators of our lives, that will be what we will see. Perception is reality. Perception being the ability to see, hear or become aware of something through the senses. And what we focus on becomes greater. This is important to remember. Each person is given the ability to choose what will be the foundation, the basis of how they live their lives.

Love or fear?

Some from positions of comfort, some with nothing. And yet it will be the same decision regardless of the circumstances surrounding them.

Love or fear?

Ordered not to emerge for at least two weeks (it most likely will be more), some would cower behind closed doors. Others would thrive taking the time to walk in nature, meditate, create art to draw in love and radiate it out. Most would vacillate between love and fear, some days grounded and some days warbling and spiraling in fear. It really depends on the day.

Connection in a time when humans are not to be coming into contact with other humans in order to save lives becomes fertile ground for creativity. Zoom groups have popped up for happy hours, free music offerings, craft circles and virtual connection. Connection being as simple as my light joining your light to create one flame. We can choose to rediscover our connection to spirit, taking religion out of it and focusing on the energy that joins all things. Spirit joins spirit. Energy comingles with energy through words read or spoken through cell phones or across the internet. People around the world are uniting as we all, together, battle an unseen enemy.

The sense of touch is heightened as awareness of people and surfaces are questioned. An invitation to be present, addressed to the world, has arrived. The invitation is to slow down, breathe, BE in this moment. A sudden nudge to expand our awareness and focus on what is here now. The uncertainty and unknowingness are uncomfortable. We don't like discomfort. Most of us avoid it at all costs. However, as Winston Churchill said during WWII "If you're going through hell, keep going." Doctors and leaders urge us to breathe, to meditate, to walk in nature to remain present, and to spend time with the people in our houses. This pandemic will pass. We get to choose how we will live through it. Circumstances are neutral; how we think about them is our choice. What will it be, love or fear? You decide.

(Footnote Rebel Society 4-9-20)

∞

Jordan Pond, Acadia National Park, Maine, June 2018

https://www.youtube.com/watch?v=K6g4841NZ6I
"Guaranteed" – Eddie Vedder

A RAINDROP

An ocean divine
Divided to express
To have experiences
Separate from the rest

A drop of love
Fell from the sky
As it fell
Forgetting why

There was no right
Or wrong way to go
It chose its path
Where it would flow

Sinking to the earth
Nourishing a tree
Or stuck in a puddle
Its choice what to be

Falling to an ocean
Lost in the masses
Or a speck in the desert
Feeding the cactus

All the while the creator
Watched seemingly above
Waiting with patience
For the return to love

A drop to ripple
Before it absorbs
Into a roaring ocean
Of a gazillion energy orbs

Will I remember
Will I see
That love was all
I was meant to be

Darlene Versak 2/1/20

The Beginning (57 Years Ago)

No one would know by looking at the neighborhood that anything was wrong. Verdant grass standing at attention cut one to two inches high interspersed with dandelions, clover and various weeds. Grass was the gymnast mat for kids' baseball, football, and tag games, absorbing the falls and tumbles. Tall maple and oak trees lined the street known as Clover Lane. One-story rancher homes built in the 1950s lined the road. Each house was exactly the same: 3 small bedrooms, 1 bath, a kitchen and a living room cut and pressed onto neatly divided lots about half an acre in size. A sandwich sliced front yard that acted as a buffer to the road and provided enough room to host a pick-up game of baseball or football. The backyard was huge. Children could be seen swinging from branch to branch in the large cherry and willow trees, sometimes hanging upside down to feel the rush of blood to their heads. On any given summer day, dares of "How high can you go?" floated above the foliage. The adults contemplated erecting fences to preserve privacy versus the freedom of having all the land invisibly seamed together. The picture on the outside was pleasant and happy. The neighborhood was evidence of the fruits of the American dream.

No one knew what went on behind closed doors.

"Keep the windows shut or the neighbors will hear you." These words were ingrained in me. My training from an early age both consciously and unconsciously was do not let others know what was really going on. Keep the picture pretty and intact. I'm not sure why my mother thought that strategy of keeping the windows closed worked. We always heard the neighbors when they were fighting. Of course, we all pretended nothing was happening unless there was a crash, bang or broken glass. Most times no one stepped in. We all obliged in the pretense that nothing had happened. As long as no one was being physically hurt, people minded their own business. This was part of the fabric of our lives. Threads woven in the background - happening, gossiped about and then forgotten until a new drama arose on Clover Lane. There was the surface story and then there was the real story - otherwise known as the truth. All kinds of murkiness, speculation and tales lay in-between.

What we feared was judgment. Judgment about our lives. Judgment about how we were living. Judgment that condemns all in its path. I didn't understand as a child the devastating effects that judgment has on lives. I only knew that it mattered to my family how we were perceived. So, the mask was carefully tended to. The mask was what you allowed the world to see while quietly, behind the scenes and under the mask, what was really going on needed to be hidden from other people. Better yet, it needed to be hidden from other people's bright interrogator light of judgment.

My next door neighbors growing up were first-generation immigrants from Italy. Move-in day began with a caravan of cars filled with family arriving behind a giant U-Haul full of possessions. We watched as a huge feast was set in motion and family helped move our new neighbors in. We didn't know it that first day, but most weekends to come, there would be a feast, full of laughter and greased with alcohol, tons of food and connection. Conversations in Italian flowed with the wine. Within a year, a long rectangular table was constructed in the backyard. Four or five smaller rectangular tables were grafted together with seats made of tree trunks carefully placed around it, creating a rustic banquet table. When a tablecloth was applied, the scene resembled the head table at a wedding. An elongated oval above ground pool with a deep end was installed that first summer as well, which ensured that the family would gather there in the sunshine and humidity to cool off and enjoy each other's company. All of the ingredients for the weekly party were put in place.

My neighbors lived life passionately. We'd been taught to hide our emotions. My neighbors were all about expressing theirs. Along with the happy feasts there were times when anger flared, and screaming and fighting could be heard several houses away. Loud emotions expressed, always captured the attention of the neighborhood. Especially after the wine had flowed for several hours; a grand battle might erupt between two men and the ferocity of the anger was a sight to behold for me. We had been taught to hide that, so watching it from my back yard was like viewing an opera… all emotions in high gear.

There was one fight I remember vividly. It didn't happen on a weekend at one of the feasts. It was an ordinary weekday. One afternoon the wife began screaming. In that moment, she didn't care about the world around her or what they thought. This screaming came from deep within her, like a wounded animal howling in the forest. Something bad had happened. Both my mother and I stopped dead in our tracks so we could listen better. We both moved to my mother's bedroom window to hear and peek out and see if there was anything to behold. She was shrieking at him at the top of her lungs and throwing multiple things at him. We couldn't see anything. However, we heard things hitting the walls. It seemed she wanted to hurt him physically the way that he had hurt her emotionally. We had no idea what she was saying - all her anger was expressed in Italian and at the top of her lungs. A battle had erupted and her angry words were punctuated by loud crashing noises. A storm seemed to be breaking around her words. He was responding, so we knew he was alive. Time stood still as we listened, fear rising as we wondered how this would end. It did end, finally, with a loud crash and him getting into his car and peeling out of the driveway. My mother and I ran over immediately to see just what had happened and to make sure she was alright.

The devastation in their living room was something that, as a child, I'd never seen before. Apparently, she'd thrown every single dish, plate and cup at him. Each had gone crashing into the wall, ceiling and floor. Broken china, ceramics and glass covered the floor. The mess that existed on that floor matched the mess that was happening in their marriage. My mother hugged her as she sobbed and I was given a trash bag and told to start cleaning up.

After that day, it was never discussed. I got the message: shit happens. Then we pretend it doesn't.

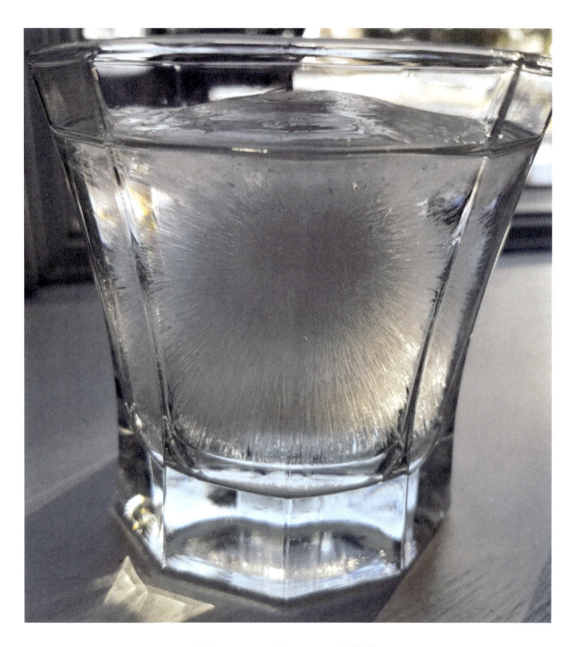

Moonwater January 2, 2018

https://www.youtube.com/watch?v=tDl3bdE3YQA

"What I Am" (Official Video) - Eddie Brickell & The New Bohemians

∞

HER SONG

Plucking on strings
Lifting notes within
Feeling my song
A sad solemn
Love song
And a happy catchy
Dance tune
Lovingly playing the chords
Creating music
Composing a life with words
Finding tone
Depth
Meaning
In words strung together
Seemingly haphazardly
Creating a symphony
Of pain described
Ecstasy desired
Worthy uncovered

DAV 4-29-16

My Childhood

I am the child of an alcoholic. That sentence used to drip in judgment for me. I have worked years to strip the condemnation and hard feelings away from that sentence. Depending on your life experience, the word "alcoholic" conjures up all kinds of thoughts, most of which center around a human being who feels helpless to fight their need for, their desire, to drink alcohol. In my case, and in the story I told myself an alcoholic was someone who drowned their sorrows with a drink. An alcoholic is an addict. I like the online dictionary's second definition of an addict: "Someone who is an enthusiastic devotee to a particular thing or activity." This definition sounds better to me. Spins the word in a way that isn't so judgmental (although I just judged the first definition, a person who is addicted to a particular substance - as boring). There is a saying in Alcoholics Anonymous (AA) that, when it comes to having a drink, one is too many and a thousand is not enough. That seems to capture the essence of it.

A complicated relationship exists when you grow up the child of an alcoholic. When I was younger, I was filled with anger and resentment toward my mother's drinking. I would think - Just stop. You need to stop! It wasn't until I went to therapy in my 20s that I learned and understood that what she does with her life is her choice. Al-Anon teaches valuable lessons. No one can be sober enough to keep anyone else sober.

What did I learn by growing up the child of an alcoholic? One of the things I learned growing up in an unpredictable household was that you never know the "what" or "why" of the drinking; you just know when a shit show has shown up inside the four walls you call home. What triggered my mother didn't matter as much as the fact that something hit a nerve. We don't want to feel that discomfort, so time to get out our go-to for making it all go away.

My mother's alcohol of preference was beer. I'm guessing she chose it because you can drink a lot of beer for a longer period of time before you wind up in wasted land.

As near as I can figure out, it seemed to go down like this. Something upset her and she'd start drinking, which meant sitting at the kitchen table with an ash tray, a pack of Kent 100s and a fresh supply of cans of liberation liquid. She'd dial up a friend and talk for hours. One cigarette after another, cloud after cloud of smoke permeated the kitchen. Gossip was shared, stories were swapped, and connection was established through the phone lines.

Sober, my mom did not fight or talk about resentments or slights that had occurred. When feelings were hurt, they entered a low simmer inside her. The alcohol would slowly raise the temperature, and all kinds of mess would boil out. She spoke her truth when she drank. She gained strength from the fire water that liberated her tongue from her internal lockdown. The alcohol freed her voice. It gave her words the brave in her needed to show up in the world - even if it was loud, disjointed and hard for all to hear. What was coming out of her was a stew of resentment that had been brewing for a long time. Once released, the prison doors quickly closed again, ready to contain the following day's slights and resentments – only to build again and await a day of venting and relief. If it was a bad night, the next day was a mixture of shame, guilt and denial that it had been that bad - that it had even happened, that all is better, just forgotten. Helplessness, no possibilities, and limited thinking pervade the thoughts of a person trained in the ways of this world. Live your own life at your own peril, for you will be alone. The great struggle we all face as humans is how shall we live? Who will be in charge of our thinking? Is it Love? Or is it fear?

LESSONS OF BEING A CHILD OF AN ALCOHOLIC

The family we choose to be born into is one of the important choices our soul makes prior to arriving. Family is one of the forces that shapes the lens with which we view the world. Our family and our experiences as babies, toddlers, children, and teenagers teach us lessons. Some lessons will be conscious; some will be unconscious. Our ego will take neutral circumstances and create stories to make sense out of it all. Stories are interesting because they can be true, untrue or have aspects of both within them. However, stories are stories. Circumstances are neutral. Our parents teach us many things, through what is spoken and also through what is unspoken. As a child, I remember watching adults with wonder…listening not just to their words, but also to their body language and their energy. Someone can be saying one thing in words, but the meaning, tone and message coming from their body can be totally different.

IT BEGINS WITH SELF-LOVE

We are love. It makes sense to me that I must love myself first, before I can ever love someone else. When I value myself, I am who I was created to be, whether or not I'm in a relationship. Be kind to yourself. I used to say, "No one is harder on me than me." It was true. I allowed others' words to hurt me, but my own words to myself were crippling.

I know my worth because I exist. Love emanates from within and begins with loving myself first. I wandered around this point for many years. I lived my life trying to do what I thought was the "right thing." But I wasn't honoring who I was created to be. I was minimizing myself; making myself small so I could fit into the nice square box of "Acceptable" that this world wants us to think is normal. I was a chameleon ready to change into what the environment expected me to be mostly to avoid conflict. I could change color, mood, and silence beliefs in an instant once I had surveyed the lay of the land and I thought I knew what was expected of me.

Witnessing another soul struggle with addiction of any kind is difficult. You want to scream, "JUST STOP!" It was only when I detached with love and allowed my mom to come to her own realization that the choice for a substance to numb out provides only temporary relief from a long running problem. Each of us must choose ourselves at some point in our lives, or not. This is where choice comes in.

I believe we're each born with a hole inside. An empty place of longing for communion with something greater than ourselves - a longing to be one with all that is. We stuff donuts and wine in our God hole, numbing out consciousness. We don't like to sit in our discomfort. We flee. We run from ourselves. Trying to hold the beach ball of truth under water just a little longer. Except we all know what happens when you hold a beach ball under water; eventually you have to let go. Then, that ball charges to the surface. We have a yearning for communion, for oneness inside. We came to this world for a purpose. It might not be grand in the world's judgment. Perhaps it's to love right where you are. It's to be the best pie maker in your county. It might be to open a restaurant and serve people food made with love. Whatever you came here to do, or to learn, if you wake up within the dream, you can play life in a different way. It's not so serious. It's knowing you're loved. It's knowing you are love. It's knowing that you can create whatever life you want by intention. It's finding your "why," and trusting that the "how" will follow.

There's a question that fascinates me: "If you knew you couldn't fail, what would you do?" Contemplate that. If you knew you couldn't fail, what would you do?

We arrive in innocence. Innocence is our natural state of being. We arrive with hearts wide open, ready to love and be loved. Our journey in life is to clear our own lens – the one we peer at the world through - and get back to innocence. With every lesson learned, and as our awareness increases, we are clearing our obstacles to Love. Or not.

A WRINKLE

A wrinkle in time
A wrinkle in my mind
You stay
Marking your place
Your space
In my life
In my heart
A knot
Holding energy
Charged with feeling
As I touch it
I feel you

DAV 11-18-17

Gloria's Story

There are all kinds of drinkers. The neighbor we shared a driveway with drank all the time. Sometimes he'd be on a bender for days. My mom usually drank one weekend night and maybe one night during the week. She felt that, because she didn't go to a bar (as her mother had), it was OK. She rationalized that she was not doing anything wrong. She'd judged the bar and determined that hanging out at a bar was wrong because that's what her mother did, and she didn't like it.

My mother was raised by her grandmother. My grandfather (who I never met because he died when my mother was 10) was named Gunnar. We were told he was dashing and handsome. He was 40-years-old when he died from an ulcer. Unfortunately, he was born at a time when science did not know how to treat those. When he died, he left my grandmother alone to raise my mother. Just prior to Christmas in 1941, my grandmother was widowed at the age of 34. She found herself having to go out into the world to work to support herself and her 10-year-old daughter. One of the ways my grandmother coped was to head to the neighborhood bar after work and unwind. All of this left my mother to be raised by my great-grandmother. I was told my great grandmother was a very loving person. I barely remember meeting her, as I was a small child the few times we visited. She died when I was 4-years-old.

My mother's alcoholism played out in the confines of her home. Because her mother drank at a bar, my mother chose to focus on location as the primary thing to judge. As long as she wasn't drinking at a bar she was fine. The fact that she was drinking out of control was a minor detail according to her logic.

As near as I can figure, and the story that I created to make sense of all this is, was that Gloria felt powerless over her life. Her escape hatch to relieve the pressure was a can of Schmidt's beer (or 10 or 12). A normal drinking evening went like this: click the tab of the can, light a cigarette and jump on the phone with a friend. The pop-tops kept clicking open. The room was a hazy cloud of smoke. Laughter and tears could be heard throughout the three-bedroom rancher house. What followed was lots of gossiping, storytelling, gobs of drama and validation that she was right. This venting of the pain did not make it go away, but the venting of it…well, that was just enough to keep going.

My mother is the first person I loved with all my heart. She taught me about love. She loved me wholly, fully and to the depth of my being. She was my first playmate. She was my first love. She was truly a character: funny, playful and beautiful. Her imagination was so fun to play with. We would set up tea parties for my dolls and stuffed animals, and I learned from her how valuable friends can be. Life, she taught me, would be disappointing at times, with heartache deposited at your doorstep when you least expect it. Having friends to support and encourage you would be a lifeline to see you through. Friends are my lifelines. Friends are people who see your shit and love you anyway.

Death – What I Was Taught – Peering Through My Lens For Death

I was playing with dolls one evening on our living room floor. I was very young and on TV, the newscasters were talking about how many people had died that day in Vietnam. It was the late 1960s and the United States was becoming more heavily involved in the Vietnam war. I turned to my mother, who was doing a Hide and Seek in her recliner chair, and asked, "What does that mean?" She responded without looking up: "That means they are going to heaven to be with God." I asked, "Do they come back?" Gloria got quiet, with eyes looking down. Without daring to look at my face, she said, "No, we'll never see them again."

In that moment, I felt immense sadness. The thought of death started to swim in my little girl brain. That's it. Never to be seen again. I asked, "Do all people die?" Still looking down at her Search and Find, she responded with one word, "Yes."

In that instant, I thought about my mother dying. Enormous pain flooded my heart. Tears filled my being. I turned away so she wouldn't see the tears I would shed in the future at the news of her death. I had already learned well not to show emotion. The memory is vivid for me. The imagined grief and loss of something that would occur in the future felt unbearable for my child brain. My ego stepped in quickly – don't think about that. She's alive. She's here now. The thought of death is one of my earliest memories. It was a conscious experience of how powerful my thoughts and imagination are.

"These thoughts do not mean anything." – Lesson 4, A Course in Miracles

Adult Version of Death – Wiping The Lens

What if we are all energy? Light having a human experience. What if we are pure love and molecules swirling, vibrating at different frequencies, shining as we will, and disguised in human bodies?

What if we choose to come here to learn, to teach, to play and, most of all, to be love?

What if this is a lesson in being an individual? We are a separate entity here (spirit living in a body), however, we are always connected to source and each other. We are not alone. We are consciousness having a human experience. We're always connected to each other and source through universal consciousness. We are co-creators of our lives. The people in our lives provide feedback. They help us uncover our blind spots, and they allow for parts of our stories to come up into our awareness in order that they may unravel and we can let them go in love.

Our childhood, teenage years and early adulthood are where we learn what the world requires of us. The rest of our time is spent unraveling the stories and programs that our families, institutions and culture have taught us, so that we find who we truly be. We return to our essence and contemplate the reason for our coming here. What is it that we came to bring uniquely to this world? We wanted to experience the contrasts of life.

There are many ways to remember who we are, and many tools are provided to find our way back to Love. Our challenge is to remember who we are. That's it! When we remember who we are, we connect to our Dharma – our life's purpose. What allows each of us to connect to Source is unique. One tool may work for you but not for me.

Because we are uniquely and wonderfully made, how we find our way on the path of returning to Love will look different for each of us. The tools I use to connect with my higher self are yoga, being in nature, hiking, meditating, writing, being a friend and focusing on breath. All of these tools remind me to slow down, be still, wake up. It is up to us whether we will heed the call to seek ourselves. The invitation is always extended. The wisdom sayings: "Seek and ye shall find," and "Ask and it will be given" are true! They are not clichés. They are words to lead the way. What is required of us is the desire to return to Love. Our willingness to follow the breadcrumb trail of spirit. That's it. It's up to us. We have the free will to choose it. It's our choice - always our choice. We are not coerced. It's our free will to choose what and how we will live our lives. We come from one consciousness: God, the Universe, a benevolent force for good, in order to have a human, separate experience, knowing that eventually, at some point in some life, we will choose to go back to one. The Universe is patiently waiting for us to choose the path of our true self. We learn here. No matter what, in pain or ease, it's our choice how we want to do it. I chose pain for a long time. I choose ease now.

All life long, we choose fear or love over and over again. When we choose judgment, fear is our choice. We are at the effect of what we judge. In other words, if I judge that all people who have short hair are dumb, I will never choose short hair because I will not want to be judged as dumb. However, if we realize that it's not my job to judge anyone else (or myself), and I recognize that all people have choices, then I am free and so are they. What other people do is simply their choice. We can change the way we look at things. Short hair becomes an interesting choice. I might not choose it, which is my choice. The fact that someone else chooses it is simply their choice. When we take the judgment out of it, it loses its charge and loosens the binding to us. We are free when we give up the role of judge in this world. Giving grace and allowing Love to be in charge - that is our choice.

I ask you again to consider that we are light. We are energy. The soul is who we are. We are a being of light who has traveled to Earth to have a human experience and learn about love. An aspect of our light is here to have the experience of being alone, separate and disconnected. That empty spot we feel inside, that's our God spot. Our spot that connects with other light beings, and ultimately, with Source. Beginning at birth, we receive programming as to how to be in this world by people who were programmed before us, and before them…and so on. We are all sons and daughters of God. Yes, God the Creator, Abba, Mother, Universe or Love, whatever name you ascribe to Source. We are ALL her children. No one is any better or worse than another. We are all equal. Period. All of us. Equal. As we grow up, we choose love or fear as the backdrop for the story that will rule our lives. To love is to not attack and so, when we choose to love, we lay down our defenses (which to the world seems insane) and trust that love has us. Our job here is to connect and love each other, to learn and to create. In love, there can be no judgment. We live at choice, allowance and possibility…and most of all, Love.

When we die, our spirit releases from this body and returns to what it is: light - pure, brilliant, glowing, shining light. We are stunning in our innocence. Our bodies die. Our spirits are immortal.

Mantra: "Universe help me in kindness to remember who I am."

Keywest – Sunset 2019 (A tear in the universe)

∞

https://www.youtube.com/watch?v=4PkcfQtibmU
"Walk" – Foo Fighters.

THE SPIDER AND THE DRAGONFLY

I was
a spider
Spinning tales
Of intrigue
Betrayal
attack
Around and around
The web
grew
until
I was
stuck
In my story
One day
A wise
Dragonfly
whispered
Drop
The stories
Surrounding
The threading
And choose
Anew
to sew
Seeds
of Love
I closed
My eyes
and fell
into
My heart
Long ago
Buried
Hidden
To avoid pain
I saw
With no
Judgment
the Beauty
Truth
Unity
And
Love
of all
that is
Now
I Create
my life

Darlene Versak 2/20/20

A love letter I wrote to myself seven years ago amidst a separation soon to be divorce. I found this in an old suitcase I was packing to go to the beach. I'm so glad I have my own back. As I read these words, I remember the courage it took to choose me.

Turn within
Silently creeping away
Don't make a peep
No one will notice
Love & light have left
The room
There are no
Genuine smiles
Only pasted on ones
For special occasions
Readied for loved ones
I can no longer be
What you think
I should be
It hurts too much
Fortify myself
Hollow footsteps
Ring on a cobblestone road
It's late
Naturally alone
I wonder
The journey within calls me
Like an old friend
This is the way
My calm waters
soothe me
With the lullaby lap
Of waves against my soul
Waves that come and dissipate
Waves that topple
Onto my shores
Gentle heart
Stay away
From the wolves
Who would tear you apart
Be strong
Hold the sparkling hope of love
In the palm of your hand
Or the seam of your pocket
Remember
Never give up
Dancing in the light
And spreading love
Is who and what
You were meant to be

Darlene Versak 7/13/19 – written in 2015

FORGIVENESS

Forgiveness
Drops
Its petals
In my heart
A gift
Given
Received
Blossoming
From
Seeds of love
Sown
In time

Sprouting up
Reaching for
Bending to
The light

The charges
Have been
dropped
The weight
Of each offense
Means nothing
Let go
Surrender
Remember who you are
Petals meant to fall.

@ Darlene Versak

Forgiveness

I chose myself. At many times in our lives, we are presented with a choice. We get to decide if we will love ourselves first. When we choose fear and judgment to run the show of our lives, the outcome is more situations, more people and more of life that is fearful and judgmental. We can choose to judge other people; however, we need to be aware that, as we give, so we receive. When I judge something or someone, I am now affected by whatever I have judged. I am at the effect of that person or thing. When I get out of the judgment game, it frees me to be whatever, to express whatever, to live however I choose to live - simply because I am free. Allowing other people and situations to be who and what they "be" opens the door to freedom for me.

First, I learned about forgiving others. I went through every nook and cranny of my mental house sweeping up the dust bunnies of unforgiveness. Mentally, I circled back to situations and people who I felt had wronged me…people I was angry with. People with whom I felt righteous indignation about. People who didn't love me the way that I wanted them to love me. And I forgave them. Forgiveness doesn't mean you condone a behavior; it means you let it go. You release the story you've been holding onto. You stop contracting and holding onto the energy of being right, of being wronged, of bunching up energetically in a knot over a person or situation. You open the door to the prison cell you created yourself with the words of a story that no longer apply. When the smoke clears, your energy flows unimpeded.

One of the bigger shadows hanging out in my mind, tucked away where no one (I thought) could see was the need and desire to forgive myself. I thought I'd be more. I thought I'd accomplish more. I wanted my life to have meaning and purpose. I'd judged my life as mediocre at best. On the surface, I could have skated along, settling. And no one would have said a thing. No one would know that I wasn't happy. I was living the middle-class American dream. Except, I wasn't happy. I wasn't being authentic. I knew the role I was to play and it was killing me. My soul had other plans. The essence I really was desired for me to wake up. The light within me had been simmering on low. Suddenly, the temperature was rising.

They say that if you put a frog in a pot of water and raise the temperature to boil, the frog won't jump out. It doesn't jump because it doesn't realize it's slowly dying. That story is what my life felt like for me. I knew I wasn't living the way I desired to live. I wasn't honoring my soul. I wasn't being the being I was created to be. Now, in that moment, I couldn't tell you that. I knew I'd gotten myself into a pickle and it was a choice point: choose yourself … or not. I'd been given this choice point over and over again for years, and I can honestly tell you that I did not choose me. I chose everyone else's happiness over mine. For me, in the middle of a mid-life depression that I felt would overtake me, I made the choice to surrender. Surrender to Love. I surrendered the life I'd carefully crafted. I surrendered so that I could live in truth. Time was running out, and I wanted whatever would come next to be honest. I desired a true relationship with myself and with other people. I desired a life of truth. I did not know what would come next. However, I trusted that Love walked beside me, and I knew that everything is figureoutable. Love had my back. Love has your back, too.

Phoenixville Firebird Festival – December 2016
https://www.youtube.com/watch?v=fyiEJaf-IzE
"If We Were Vampires" - Jason Isbell and the 400 Unit

LONGING

I desire
the kind of Love
That knows my heart
And feels my soul
For eyes that see
Through the disguise
And no matter what
Wants to be
Next to me
For hands that know
A gentle caress
And when to pull
A body tightly
A vibration
That resonates
To the tune
Of passion
And peace
I desire to be
Alive

Darlene Versak 10/20/20

Redemption

noun

1. *an act of redeeming or atoning for a fault or mistake, or the state of being redeemed.*

2. *deliverance; rescue.*

3. *Theology. Deliverance from sin; salvation.*

4. *Atonement for guilt.*

5. *Redeem*

6. *to make up for; make amends for; offset (some fault, shortcoming, etc.):*

His bravery redeemed his youthful idleness.

7. to *obtain the release or restoration of, as from captivity, by paying a ransom.*

8. *Theology. to deliver from sin and its consequences by means of a sacrifice offered for the sinner.*

I was given a shot at redemption. It was a chance to make a perceived wrong, right. It was an opportunity to atone for the guilt of having thrown away a living thing. The story I posted in the closed writing group was about wild flowers in a vase that had died, but the roots had begun to grow and they were still alive. I struggled to let it go. If the roots still had life, shouldn't I keep them? In my story, the decaying flowers were a metaphor for my marriage, and in the end, I put the flowers in the trash and ended my ordeal of trying to keep them alive. So it was in life as well.

I met two new writer friends from our group for dinner. One of my friends gave me two essentially dead plants. It was a joke. The two containers had been left outside and were full of leaves and debris. There was not enough soil in each pot, and it was difficult to see if there was even anything left alive. He was giving me a chance to redeem myself. When I explained the meaning of the piece I'd written, he felt bad. "Just throw them out" he said. "I would."

See but I couldn't. There is something inside of me that just doesn't give up. I should. I take too long to come to the decision. But if there is life, if there is a chance at life, I will try. I will love someone or something back into existence if they let me. I will try anyway. Until I don't. Until I won't. Until I'm done. I collect people and I love them. It's who I am. I see the beauty in people, in life that others would throw away, maybe because I always felt like a throw away.

I got to work when I got home and assessed the situation. Two containers were given to me, one larger than the other. In the large container there were a couple leaves on the plant that looked like it might still be alive. I just need to resuscitate this one. The smaller container had few visible signs of life: a little color existed at the base of one of the rotting plants. First, gently remove the dead leaves that had fallen into the pot from nearby trees and as much debris as possible and water the plants. Their new home would be my front window, which gets sunlight all morning. I put the two dying plants in my front window; it seemed to fit my mood.

I watered them once a week, carefully draining the pots of excess water and gently placing them back in their window spot. The first couple of weeks it was questionable, whether there was anything still alive in the smaller pot, but gradually, new shoots erupted from the soil. The larger plant responded right away to care and attention. I realized these plants, were indeed, still alive. I added more soil. I talked to them. I played music. The plants came back to life.

Does my loving these plants redeem me? My world is thick with symbols, signs and hidden meaning. From a perceived death comes life. Have I atoned for mistakes made? Have I paid the price for letting go? Too many questions arise, but they always do for me. What is my lesson with these plants? Hope is alive. Love is a powerful energy.

Today I sit with my morning coffee and marvel at two beautiful plants growing rich in meaning.

DAV 12-31-15

∞

https://www.youtube.com/watch?v=XlCSW2ICJjQ&list=PL3Cd0hP_ZoA3fXVGxhj2Vd3Ic6GcHOFdc

"Every Time I Hear that Song" – Brandi Carlisle

San Francisco Sunset June 15, 2014
https://www.youtube.com/watch?v=Ux7HgO9QhAc
"That's The Way I Always Heard It Should Be" – 1971 – Carly Simon

UNRAVELING

Unraveling
like ribbon
Strewn across the table
Rolling toward the unknown
Round and round we go
Tangled in tension

The unraveling must end
Coming apart at the seams
At some point
It's finished
Pieces torn apart
Tattered bits remain
Carefully unknotted
The last whole ribbons
Let them fall to the floor
Sweep the tangled mess up
Throw it in the trash
It's over
It's over
It's over

D. Versak 2016

The Flicker of Discontent

I felt the flicker of discontent while having lunch at Panera Bread 15 years ago. It would be 8 years before I did anything about it. I chose my sensible "you-pick-two" lunch made up of chicken noodle soup (a low calorie choice), Greek salad minus the pepperoncini and onions (no bad breath for me, thank you), French bread (my favorite part of the lunch, as I love to slather three pats of butter onto the 3-inch long bread, which negates all my previous prudent choices) and a small cup of water that I squeeze two lemons into (because they are counting on your laziness to not want to get up and refill that small cup so just buy a drink already, Cheap Ass; but no, it's really more about the unwanted calories anyway). My single friend Lisa was talking about her love life, and that's when I felt it. My soul was sending me signals via soul speak; you know, the language of the soul. Suddenly I felt profound sadness. The loudness of people noisily chatting next to us and all around us evaporated, and I was completely still. Like a movie when time stops for everyone else except the main character, I wasn't in Panera's anymore - I just…was. I stared out the window at the blur that had become the parking lot and the message was clear: you feel empty; you feel alone. Do something! Wake up!

It startled me. It scared me. What? I do? Shit, shit, shit! The picture I showed the world was almost perfect. People thought my family was beautiful. I had a great marriage. My kids were so kind and well mannered. What the fuck is wrong with me? See, that's just the thing, isn't it? It was a picture. Oh, it wasn't a terrible facade. But for me, I was disappearing. I was fading into the picture.

"Hey, where are you?" Lisa asked. Immediately all sensations returned, and I looked her straight in her puzzled chestnut eyes. The noisiness of the place restored, and I transported back to the now.

"Are you alright? Is everything OK?" she asked. She meant it, this question; she saw that I had gone somewhere, if only for seconds.

"Have you ever felt alone in the world?" I asked her pensively. That was the beginning…I see it now.

The 3:00 am Call From My Soul To Wake The Fuck Up

Whispers came in the deep night at first. Tiny longings in such a small voice, it was difficult to hear. Gradually, the voice, when it realized I was actually listening; became stronger, it knew that I wanted to hear it. Or maybe I was focusing on it versus burying it. It had been so long since I paid attention. Would I really come back to myself and hear words to set me back on my path? I wondered where had this voice been all these years. I knew - I had stuffed it down, smothered it, not allowed myself to feel, really feel, anything. I was safe. I was doing what was right, what was necessary. I knew what my role was supposed to be: be a good wife, a selfless mother, a responsible person, volunteer, help others. But who was helping me? I thought I wanted those roles; I thought that was what my life was supposed to be. And yet something didn't feel right. If this was the life I was supposed to be living then why? Why had the yearning started? The "3 and 4 o'clock in the morning wake up and know that your life is not your own" anxiety. I was living a script, not what I wanted, not my desires; someone else's story. Somehow I'd allowed what was expected of me to take over, going through each day unconsciously, completing tasks, crossing off items on the to-do list. Until one day, I realized that I had been sleepwalking through life. My life was not mine anymore. I had handed over control to circumstances outside of myself. It's not the life I intended to live. Holy shit, how did this happen? I've been asleep at the wheel. What am I going to do?

Horseshoe Canyon Sunset 6-25-17

https://www.youtube.com/watch?v=PciJq0qYJj8

"How Can You Mend A Broken Heart" (Live in Las Vegas 1997 – One Night Only)

– Bee Gees

WABI SABI LOVE

I am
a wabi sabi
work of art
Impermanent
Imperfect
Incomplete
Broken pieces
Fused in golden pathways
Of love

Light lives
Glowing inside
Cracks and holes
Left by loss
Shining
Attracting
Being

Time's patina
Wrinkles, spots and soft folds
Accentuate this
Vessel
Of light

Stories of
Triumph
and
Tragedy
Written in each scar
A patchwork of beauty
Lies in
Quilted pieces
Reverently assembled
As love
Breathes in me

Darlene Versak © 2-5-19

The Song on The Radio

He arrived so that we could pay the bills, one of the last tasks that we still did together. The house would be sold in June, as soon as our son graduated from high school. We were doing the right thing by our kids. We'd decided at the end of his 10th grade year to separate. I would stay in the house, and, every other weekend, I would leave and go to my sister's so that he could spend the weekend with the boys. We were very amicable toward one another. Neither of us understood why people tore each other apart like lions fighting over fresh meat when they left each other; we wanted to remain friends. We'd spent 22 years together and it meant something. It was the beginning of our divorce, October of my youngest son Jackson's senior year. My soon-to-be ex-husband had a girlfriend now. He seemed happier and busier. I really didn't talk to him except for matters having to do with the kids or the investment property we shared. The divorce papers had been served earlier that week, and in 90 days it would finally be official: we would be divorced.

He had asked earlier in the week to please account for the mortgage payment when I got paid. Originally, I'd planned to give him $600. I lived close to the line. My checking account had a $100-dollar minimum balance, and after I got paid and divvied up the money, I usually hovered around $125 - just enough to avoid the below balance fee. Two weeks ago, however, I'd paid (via check) my yearly bill for LA Fitness ($259), which would grant me unlimited visits to any LA Fitness for the next 12 months. The problem occurred when the bank cashed the same check twice. I'd noticed it when I looked at my online statement to see the exact amount I was being paid that week. I saw check #275 for $259 as one entry as a check, and on the very next line, a debit charge for $259 with the same check number noted. I'd already bounced two checks and was hit with overdraft charges. Fuck. After sorting through what needed to be done and going to the bank to fill out a denial for the debit charge, the resolution was that it would be 10 days before the vanished money would return to my account.

He walked in and we said hello. I was in a good mood. I'd solidified plans with my friend Sandy and would be spending the Friday of my adventure weekend sleeping at her house. I knew we would laugh all night long.

"What are your plans again on Sunday?" he asked.

"I'm headed to Brooklyn for a flea market with Jacque and Sharon. I'm not sure what time I'll be back; I'll probably miss Jackson's soccer game." I knew I would miss the game and didn't know what time I'd really be home.

"What do you need at a flea market in Brooklyn?"

"I don't know. Nothing. I just want to have the experience." I loved to see the vintage pieces, the creative inventions of crafters, the art of the entire experience. Plus, it was an adventure in New York. The adventure drew me in.

"You know I got paid today and I have $500 to give you toward the mortgage." I started.

He seemed irritated. "I thought you'd be giving me $600."

"Well, that had been the plan, but the bank fucked that up when they double cashed my LA Fitness payment, so I'm short this week. They said it should be back in my account within 10 business days and it's been five as of today. As soon as the money returns, I'll write you a check for $100. Can you spot me till that happens?"

"And you're going to Brooklyn?" he questioned.

"Yup." I responded.

Now he turned and faced me square. "How ya going to live, Darlene? When this is over - and it'll be over before you know it. How you gonna live?" He asked with anger in his voice.

"I don't know," I answered truthfully. The whimsy of my upcoming adventure was quickly losing some sparkle.

"Prayer isn't going to be the magic answer this time," he retorted.

"I don't know. It's worked for me in the past. Somehow, I always wind up OK," I answered slowly. My confidence was sinking in the sand. The impending fun of my Friday night and Sunday New York adventure was suddenly and abruptly called into question.

"I don't mean to rush you, but I need to get the kids dinner," he said. "Are you ready to leave? I need you to move your car."

"OK, yeah, like you don't mean to rush me, whatever." Now I was mad.

The land I was standing on previously had suddenly dissolved. I was sinking. How was I going to live? I'd have an electric bill, water, sewer, internet, and phone bill - in addition to a mortgage or rent - and I could barely scrape together that money. Fear and anger rose to the surface. Man, why'd he have to be so mean about it. What the fuck? I was pissed and scared at the same time.

I went back in the house and finished gathering my clothes and suitcase for the weekend. Every time I came down the stairs, it seemed I remembered something else to run back up to find. A book to read for Saturday when I had no plans, grab a bottle of wine to bring with the rotisserie chicken and Caesar salad for dinner tonight. I packed up my trunk went back into the house for my sunglasses and came out of the house just as he pulled in the driveway behind me with dinner for the kids.

He smiled, "Perfect timing."

I got in the car, and the song on the radio was How Can You Mend a Broken Heart by The Bee Gees. It had just begun. In that moment, it was decided - I needed to know. He reversed out of the driveway backing to the left; I backed out to the right. I would pass him directly, with the song played in the background. I pulled up beside him and rolled down the window. "Do you hate me?" I asked. I looked into his green eyes, the ones I'd searched so many times over the years looking for love, looking for truth. He smiled.

"No, I don't hate you. I love you. You're a good person."

I was shocked. It surprised me. A vibration went through my soul. He was telling the truth.

"Why would you say that?" he asked.

"Because you were mean to me earlier," I replied.

"I'm speaking the truth, Darlene. There is a reality to your situation. You're going to need to face it."

He wished me happiness and was genuinely concerned for my well-being. He'd moved on. He wasn't in love with me either. He loved me as a human being, and that was all.

The song continued in the background. "We could never see tomorrow, no one said a word about the sorrow."

Tears gathered behind my eyes. I looked at him. "I love you, too." Before the tears began to fall, I drove away with the song reaching the crescendo: "Please help me mend my broken heart, and let me live again."

The text appeared before I reached Sandy's house. It read: "I'm sure you know, but just to be clear. I don't hate you. I want to see you be happy in whatever you do." And I knew for sure that it was over. I was sad, but it was OK. I would be OK.

DAV 11-2-15

∞

Dinner at Pho Thai Nam, East Norriton, PA 2017

https://www.youtube.com/watch?v=4NPAz8-O29U

"Alfie" – Dionne Warwick

∞

Alfie

She told me I was brave. She also said that, at first, she thought I was crazy. Maybe the two go hand in hand? When I first told Dottie (my older neighbor across the street) I was getting a divorce, she wondered, "What the hell does she want? He's a good man; he's handsome, she has a beautiful home and two smart, kind and handsome boys. She has more than most people would dream of, and yet…she wasn't happy?"

Dottie confessed that now she understood. "It was your heart, your yearning to be happy. Most people would have settled. Not you, Alfie!"

I remembered the song (sort of) from childhood. I remembered only one line: "What's it all about, Alfie?" I made a mental note, Google the lyrics to that song.

I thanked her for her encouraging words. I had questioned myself continuously over the last year, and every time the answer still came up the same: your heart is not in this anymore. My heart pounded me awake. I couldn't go back to who I was before and I wasn't sure what the crystal ball future looked like. I only knew that I was moving into a new life. It reminded me of the scene in the Matrix when Morpheus tells Neo, "You take the blue pill – the story ends. You wake up in your bed and believe whatever you want to believe. You take the red pill - you stay in Wonderland and I show you how deep the rabbit hole goes." Did I want to know truth? My truth? Would I heed my hippie heart?

I, like Neo, took the red pill. And the adventure continues.

Alfie
By Burt Bacharach

What's it all about, Alfie?
Is it just for the moment we live?
What's it all about when you sort it out, Alfie?
Are we meant to take more than we give
Or are we meant to be kind?
And if only fools are kind, Alfie,
Then I guess it's wise to be cruel.
And if life belongs only to the strong, Alfie,
What will you lend on an old golden rule?
As sure as I believe there's a heaven above, Alfie,
I know there's something much more,
Something even non-believers can believe in.
I believe in love, Alfie.
Without true love we just exist, Alfie.
Until you find the love you've missed you're nothing, Alfie.
When you walk let your heart lead the way
And you'll find love any day, Alfie, Alfie.

Finally, I Choose Me

Our lives have many twists and turns. Things happen that we have no control over. People get sick, we lose jobs, a mate betrays us, a tornado barrels down your street. Through all of this, we get to decide if we will choose ourselves. I used to wonder what people meant when they said, "You have to love yourself." What exactly did that look like? Pedicures, massages, new clothes? I wondered, "What does that statement actually mean?"

In the process of getting divorced, I learned exactly what that meant. I began a deep relationship with and learned to love myself. I spent time - lots of time - alone. The time spent was not in loneliness. I decided to view the time spent as if I were dating myself. I became re-acquainted with Darlene. What are my desires? What do I want? What kinds of things do I like? Earlier in life, at 27, after two years of intense therapy (individual and group) and living on my own for the first time for a year, I had found myself. I thought my work was done. The funny thing about working on and being in a relationship with yourself is it's a process that doesn't end. I had finished therapy. I'd firmly taken my power back. At that point, I thought I'd "graduated." I had cleared my childhood trauma and thought that was it.

Soon, I met a wonderful man, fell in love, got married and proceeded to "lose" myself all over again. I didn't realize that if you don't continue to have a relationship with yourself, if you neglect yourself, you lose touch with who you "be" and your voice is quieted. I found myself going along to get along. I lost myself in the marriage, in being a parent, in following the script handed to me as a child. I could say it was having children, I could say it was the grind of keeping a roof over our heads. I could say it was lots of things. But, at the end of the day, I take accountability for the choices I made and decisions not to speak up. Those choices were mine.

Just as in any relationship, having a relationship with yourself takes time, attention and effort. It is a lifelong love affair.

CHOOSING ME

You will be given many opportunities to choose yourself in life. Sometimes you will, sometimes you won't. I do know that, whether it's in this life or the next or the next, eventually you will choose you. You will choose to love yourself first.

What I Learned From Grief

Everything is temporary. Let's start with that. Everything. This walking in quicksand. This every-fucking-step-is-heavy feeling will end. The urge to cry when someone who sincerely cares about you asks how are you will pass. When I'm bogged down, when I can't find the light switch, that is the hardest time to remember that this, too, shall pass. At the other end, when you are on top of the mountain, in that very moment, hold it, breathe it in and solidify it in your memory. Because there will surely come a day when you will be at the bottom of a ditch, and you'll need to know that the mountain is there and you will be on top again. It's just a matter of time. In the meantime, when moving in any direction feels like sinking, remember to breathe and just keep moving … one step at a time.

I wasn't prepared for the grief of my divorce. I grieved for a solid two and a half years. I felt profound sadness every day. But I kept going. I took one step, then another, living in this 10 minutes, then the next 10 minutes, then the next and so on till I'd strung together a full day. I heard a definition for grief that I think captures the essence of it:

"Grief, I've learned, is really just love. It's all the love you want to give but cannot. All that unspent love gathers up in the corners of your eyes, the lump in your throat, and in that hollow part of your chest. Grief is just love with nowhere to go." - Jamie Anderson

I hardly gave myself permission to cry. I had a story, a program from my childhood about crying that I learned about and allowed to be released through the transformation work I began during the divorce. I'd been taught in childhood to hide emotions. Emotions show your heart. Emotions show how vulnerably human you are. My mother didn't like to see me cry. She didn't like to see anyone cry. I learned at an early age to hide under my bed when I needed to cry. Vivid memories of carpet wet with tears rise up every now and again when the urge to cry presents itself.

Emotions are carried by water that boils up inside us. Our emotions overflow through our eyes which releases them. Tears are necessary. They're cleansing. But hell, I hated having puffy eyes. Usually, I fought it, steadfast in my determination not to fuck up my face for the day. Cry at night? That actually seemed to make it worse. I would wake up and the visage in the mirror looked like I'd been in a fight and my eyes had lost the round. They'd been punched by grief. Eyelids heavy with water weight, inflamed with the pain of too many tears forced out in the emotional release the night before. Once I allowed the tear ducts to open, a deluge would result because they had been closed for too long. My tear ducts didn't want to turn off. It seemed that when I allowed the tears to flow, they didn't want to stop. The tears kept filling my eyelids for a while, hence the puffiness.

I'd been living a half-life, not taking chances, afraid to lose, afraid to risk, afraid to truly live. I didn't demand what I wanted. Hell, I didn't even ask for it. I took what I got like a caged animal and passively accepted what was given. I longed to love fully, to dare fully, and to swing for the fences again. There is a price to pay for living authentically. Passion requires payment. To live in the moment, to fully be alive, requires all of you. Most of all, it requires you to be present. For each of us, what we must surrender is different. So is what we must offer. We can't avoid conflict. We can't be nice. We can't subjugate our needs for others. We have to choose ourselves for a change. I had to speak my truth with love, but I still had to speak it. For me, I put everyone and everything else above my wants and my needs. So, for me to be real, I had to find my voice and speak my truth. It was hard. I decided it was time to practice courage. When I consistently practice courage, I become competent at courage, and competence is a short walk to confidence. The beginning is rough, but determination allows it to get easier the more you do it.

Walking through the fire melts away the bullshit. Melts away what doesn't matter. When everything has been pushed down and denied, to change seemed the scariest thing in the world. I had changed once before - I had gotten a hold of my life 25 years ago. I'd gone to therapy, did a lot of work on myself, and I thought I'd graduated and was done. But over time, I slipped back into my unconscious slumber - not wanting to rock the boat, always wanting to keep the peace. But the voice inside - your soul - it doesn't give up on you. You may give up on you, but who you really are, the real in you, doesn't give up on you-EVER. It whispers to you at night, at work, in the car and in any quiet moment. It shouts at you in your dreams: WAKE UP!

Your whole life is about waking up. It's about being real. It's about living your truth whatever that is. Courage is required. When I separated from my ex-husband, I began to practice courage on purpose. I purposely did things that scared me, so that I could face my fears. I started hiking and faced my fear of heights. I still have a fear of heights, but it no longer stops me from doing what I love which is hiking on trails and getting to the top of mountains. Every time I practice courage, it reinforces my bravery.

My truth and my lessons are different from yours, or maybe they're similar it doesn't matter. All that matters is being in the present moment, walking with intention speaking your dreams and what you really think with kindness, and fully experiencing who you are. You are precious and the world needs YOU, the you that you were created to be.

∞

Puerto Adventuras, Mexico – January 17, 2020

https://www.youtube.com/watch?v=5r6A2NexF88

"The Joke" (Official Video) – Brandi Carlile

WE ARE ONE

We are they
They are we
One we be
Witnessing a
Staggering tragedy

Our sisters are crying
Our brothers are dying
Senselessness surrounds
Truth and Light
shine on
shadows
there is no denying

Winners and losers
Cards handed at birth
In a world
Where judgment and fear
Determine your worth

The day arrives
A choice
must be made
What will it be

Love or fear

that rules my heart
And guides my mind

Love melts
The fog of ignorance
Shrouding this world

The choice is mine

We were lost
Now
we are found

Forgiveness, kindness, mercy abound
Remember
who you are
A warrior for love
Or worrier of the world

Remember
the love you came to give
And receive

Together we walk home
Together we rise

@Darlene Versak 6/5/20

Equality

George Floyd was murdered while in police custody on May 25, 2020. In a video lasting 8 minutes and 46 seconds, I watched a human being be ignored as he pleaded "I can't breathe" over 16 times in 5 minutes. He called for his momma just before he died. Tears ran down my face. My stomach turned and I wanted to look away. A blatant disregard for human life was captured on video and then traveled around the world, igniting a movement against racism.

After the video went viral, there were peaceful protests as well as looting and rioting. The two groups are not together; they are different. One group is seeking change through non-violent means and the other group is seeking change through violence. Love or fear is the choice again. Things need to change, and there are two ways to go about that change: a violent way or a non-violent way. That video woke me up. I cannot stand by as my brothers and sisters are treated differently.

I saw in that video man's inhumanity to man. It has happened before and it will happen again - unless we are diligent and stay awake to the forces of power and division that try to separate us in this world. A spotlight shined on the actions of four police officers that day, uncovering the systemic problem of racism that exists. It caused me to look at myself. It made me look at and contemplate where I, as a White person, enjoyed White privilege.

I consider myself to be a spiritual person. When the Black Lives Matter movement started, I thought, "Well, all lives matter." At the time, I didn't recognize that statement as spiritual bypass. In his book, Toward a Psychology of Awakening," John Welwood defines spiritual bypass as, "…spiritual ideas and practices to sidestep personal, emotional 'unfinished business,' to shore up a shaky sense of self, or to belittle basic needs, feelings, and developmental tasks." The underpinning of it is avoidance or repression. We spiritually bypass because we don't want to actually face the situation.

My religion is love and truth. So, what is the truth? The truth in our country is that Black people are treated differently than White people and, until we acknowledge it, educate ourselves, change the systems themselves and end the denial, nothing will change. The first step, as anyone in AA will tell you, is to admit that there is a problem

∞

https://www.youtube.com/watch?v=TlFCfkyuQM0
"Everybody" – Ingrid Michaelson

I Am as God Created Me (Lesson 94, 162, 176) – A Course in Miracles (ACIM)

God/Love created the world and all that's in it. God did not create any people less than any other people. We are all created equally in love. I was conceived in love. I was born with the natural inclination to love. Who I become is part nature (who I was created to be) and nurture (who I was taught to be). The world in which we live - the country, state, culture and our family, all contribute to the ideas that each of us have as to who we are. The lens with which we view the world is skewed by many contributing factors.

I believe that God/Universe/Source is love. I believe that I was created by God. I am as God created me. Therefore, I am love. Period. My essence, my soul is love. We use our five senses to perceive what is real in this world. Overall, I want to see it to believe it. However, our senses deceive us. Images betray truth. What is real and what is true can get lost in misdirection, story, denial and distraction.

Man's search for meaning brings us to the question that haunts everyone here: Why? Why am I here? Why is this happening? Why pain? Why change? Why suffering? Why?

What if it's simple. I am love. I came from love. You are love. You came from love. We are all love. Now I hear the interruption. Umm, excuse me - not all people are love. Some people are chaos and destruction. Here's the beautiful thing: I also came here with free will, better known as choice. I get to choose how I will live. I get to create my life. I'm free. You're free. We're all free. I make choices and think thoughts that propel me down a road. The great thing is, at any point, we can choose differently. It's never too late to change your life. Change your story, change your life. It's never too late to be still, to listen to the voice within, and to choose differently. We can choose to unravel our stories. We can align our spirit with source (Love) at any time. We can, in an instant, change our lives.

Life can be simple. In the Bible, Jesus says in the New Testament that all of the commandments and all of the rules to live by can be boiled down to two: 1) Love God; and 2) Love each other. That's it. Two simple rules to live by. If you are not a Christian, every religion in the world holds the tenet of the Golden Rule in some form - to treat people the way that you want to be treated. Everything you do in life and everyone you meet can be held up against this rule. Am I, in this moment, expressing love to God or love to my fellow human? Period. We make things complicated. The mind likes a complex puzzle. However, God is simple. God is love..

https://www.youtube.com/watch?v=0wBDDAZkNtk
"Who Will Save Your Soul" - Jewel

ABRACADABRA

Molecules dance
To the rhythm
Of my words

Stories spoken
By lips
Unknowing

Each Letter
Formed
Thought
Spoken
Has power

Bringing to life
Lessons
To be learned

Sometimes
Over and
Over

Actors cast
In scripts
Validating illusions

Artists
Breathe life
Into
Endless
Creations

Wake up
Beautiful
Dreamer

Love
Awaits
Your return

D. Versak 7/2/19

Writing My Sage

I doubt I'll ever know. What exactly happened in that relationship? I mean, I can analyze it logically, come up with different scenarios that answer the call to figure out another's actions. But to be 100% sure, I will never know. I guess it's the mystery of it all that baffles me. Dysfunctional lives. Honesty has left the room; fear exists on both sides of exposing too much of our vulnerable. Yes, this feels familiar. I've moved to protection mode now. I started in my all-out "love everyone, love conquers all" mode and have been slammed to the ground by fear and rejection. Everything shut down… for a while. At least, that's what happened to me. I put myself out there, a flower in the wind. When the tempest built to a crescendo, I finally bowed to the ground in supplication. My intentions were pure, love the aim. My naïveté is once again to blame.

I think I'm learning. I guess I am. I hope I am. I mean, if you're in the garden, you're going to get dirty, right? If I want to be a waving flower, I have to live in the dirt awhile to make that happen. I have to stand up and ask for what I want if I want to get it. Passion is my guiding principle; I need to feel it or I'm not doing it. Writing is probably the most passionate thing I'm involved in presently. I sit at my keyboard and click my heart onto a screen and read, cry and feel whatever I'm describing that day. I feel the release of emotions and the revelation of truth. I create for myself. I write to express how I feel. Life happens and I write about it; epiphanies arrive as if on cue. When I censor myself, I wonder, "Why? What part of my voice am I hiding? Why don't I want anyone to see? Am I ashamed? Embarrassed? Why?" Writing is therapy for me. I write from deep within, and inspiration whispers meaning to me. The demons dance in my words - at least the ones I won't share out loud. The shadow has an outlet. Sometimes there are lessons to learn, sometimes feelings are shared, and sometimes it is purely a venting.

My heart had been afraid to venture out again. But I will venture out. I must. "Never give up" is one of my mantras. It's time to start again. That's where I am in life: starting over. I am literally writing myself alive. I was sleepwalking for a bit while I raised my kids. Now it's time to wake up. Each day at 5:15 a.m., I sit down and write. Some days it flows and goes. Some days I'm staring at the white walls, combing through my brain for a nugget of inspiration. Either way, I come back each day and begin again. Some days I'm happy with a creation and some days I think it's shit. Still, I create. Because it's only through practice, it is only through doing, that I will get better. Writing, for me, is how I hear my soul speak. There is a connection through my heart that opens and allows the words to flow. I think there is a channel to the Divine that lives within each of us. It's a link to a higher wisdom that I tap into when I connect with my keyboard. Some people experience this through dance, or painting, or whatever creative outlet allows them to express feelings. I've had beautiful moments of sacred when writing - when truth is flowing.

The wind dies down and I lift my head, searching for the sun. The sun warms my bright purple petals. Love give us peace. I will rise again, for that is what wildflowers do. They exist in the most unlikely places, and they stand tall in the sunlight. There is beauty in truth and I will keep searching for truth, all the while dropping seeds of love along the way.

6-16-16 DAV

If You Want to Change The World, It Starts With Yourself

I've done a lot of work to clear my lens. Spit shine, Windex, showing up, feeling, and feeling again the pangs of feeling out of alignment (flow), of knowing deep inside that something doesn't feel right. Turning my time, energy and attention to contemplate; what is happening in my body, in my life? Feeling triggered and looking at what happened. Sitting in the discomfort and asking, "Why the pain? Why the discomfort? Where is the unease coming from?" There is work to be done to clear our lens. It is true for me and it is true for you. It's true for everyone here. A shift of energy from your mind (fear) to your heart (love). The heart was intended to be the master of the mind. The ego could work for you or you could place it in control of you. We have free will. We live at choice. Freedom begins when we start to examine our thoughts. When we attack another, we attack ourselves. We are creating our lives with our thoughts all the time. As we speak, so we create. Abracadabra! Magic words used by magicians.

ACIM Lesson #196: "It can be but myself I crucify" (pages 374 & 375): "Until this shift has been accomplished, you cannot perceive that it is but your own thoughts that bring you fear, and your deliverance depends on you." Our thoughts are cloaked in defense mechanisms, designed to keep us safe from attack. Our ego wants to keep us safe. That's its job. Safety (don't put your hand in the fire) can be good. However, fear binds us. Fear limits us. Fear brings constriction. What we really fear is our strength and freedom. Marianne Williamson said, "Our deepest fear is not that we are inadequate. Our deepest fear is that we are powerful beyond measure." -- A Return to Love: Reflections on the Principles of A Course in Miracles

You came here to feel the feels - all of them. The emotions we've judged as good and the ones we've judged as bad. Yes, all of them. This is a world of contrast. You are in earth school and the curriculum is love. Subjects (to name a few) taught here are surrender, trust, forgiveness, patience, gratitude, service, and kindness. They all fall under the umbrella of love. You can put fear in charge and crucify yourself, or you can put love in charge and redeem yourself. The choice is yours.

What God Have You Made?

Is it a god of love or a god of fear? How you think, so shall it be. You are creating your life every second. Your choices provide the backdrop - the themes - that will play out in your experiences. What images do you have for God? Years ago, when I was participating in a Bible study, I said to the facilitator that there seemed to be two Gods in the Bible. My perception was that in the Old Testament, God was a God of judgment, and in the New Testament, there was a God of love. However, they are the same God. I had a hard time reconciling the differences. I see the importance of viewpoint. Who is telling the story? As the reader, what am I drawing on from my past that adds colors to the words?

When I was in college, I took a course titled "Comparative Religions" and read Siddhartha (the story of Buddha). I found the book to be a beautiful story about love. Siddhartha was a spiritual seeker who experienced an abundance of what life had to offer. He was part of the royal family, so he had luxury and riches. However, he experienced an emptiness inside. He decided to go on a quest to seek truth. He'd been shielded from the realities of everyday life. He saw that life was full of suffering when he ventured out in the world. One day, as he sat by the Bodhi tree and meditated on peace and truth, he achieved enlightenment to become the Buddha. His realization was that we are all one.

What about people who don't believe in God? I would say for people who've made that choice, there is some code that they live by. There is some framework from which they operate in this world. Whether you choose the Golden Rule or "survival of the fittest" or "all out for number one," you live with some guiding principle that directs your decisions. You can create a god out of seeking power, money or fame. You can also create a god of kindness, truth and love. Whatever your god is, you have chosen it from the multitude of possibilities available to each of us through the gift of free will. We get to choose in each minute how we will live our lives and who will hold the power.

A Dandelion's Sacred Geometry - Plymouth Meeting, PA August 2020

https://www.youtube.com/watch?v=7ifs2R7BbAk

"Love You to Life" (Official Video) – Lara Hope & the Ark Tones

Romantic Love

Love inspires our lives. Romantic love breathes new energy into our days. When we fall in love, everything dreary falls away. We feel the rush and excitement of possibility. Our senses are enlivened. The world is born anew. Oh, we feel. We feel on top of the world when we're in that person's company. We feel like we can do anything. The world crackles with excitement. Electricity fills the air. Possibilities seem endless. The mystery of getting to know the other, the allure of the unknown. Words can neither capture nor tame the wild feeling in our heart.

You might cast aside the script of your life. You might peel the layers of "should" off and run away. Love is boundless and freeing. Anything is possible when you're in love. The script and programming disintegrate in the newness of the present moment. The only thing that matters is being with your beloved. Maybe that's just it: we are wholly present with our beloved, living in the moment, for the moment. Especially in the beginning, each second is sacred. Love wakes our heart up from its drowsy sleep. The litany of the ego's endless lists, worries and fears fall to the ground. Being in the other's company - that is what is desired. For, in that time, there is no time. We are in flow. We feel the limitlessness of our being. We know all things are possible.

Again And Again – A Fable For This time

Again and again, the news breaks and spews forth stories of destruction. The daily spoonful of negativity to keep the spirit down, energy vibrating low. Lives violently ended or forever changed. There's something wrong here; there can be no denying it.

The weed of fear sprouted in the garden, in the dark, and began to spread. Love watched and allowed his sons and daughters to choose how to live, in love or fear. Choice is their superpower.

The weeds in the garden brazenly stand in the light. They've grown so large. They no longer hide. Why hide? So many have forgotten their true nature of innocence, kindness, love and truth. Shamelessly, they override the good, the holy and the beautiful.

The roots go wide and deep; dividing the good, separating the One into this side and that side, creating the illusion of separation. There is talk of "they," "the other," "us" and "them." Still, it doesn't change the truth. We are one - brothers and sisters tearing each other apart. Looking into the eyes of the false other, I see myself. It is a mirror.

The sun shines away the clouds of confusion and lies. The haze lifts. We know it's time - time to dig deep and upheave the roots sewn a long time ago by a few who would be king and hold dominion over all. It's time to rototill the earth and start with level ground, fresh with equality, possibility and love.

Hills Creek Lake, Tioga County PA 2020

https://www.youtube.com/watch?v=Vd6zYQPCgsc

"We May Never Pass This Way Again" – Seals & Crofts

The Invitation

We are energy having a human experience. Here to explore love in all its variations, in all its magnificence. Creation is our work. The invitation is simple: will you choose to wake up? Will you unravel the programming, the script of what it means to be alive on this planet at this time? Will you turn within, explore your wounds, find your shadows and walk through them, feel them in order to let them go? Will you educate, elevate and liberate your spirit? It will require practicing courage. The more consistently we practice courage, the more competent we get at it. When we consistently practice courage, our competence at facing fear turns into confidence. And before we realize it, we are brave. With each step we take toward thinking and feeling for ourselves, we become more and more of who we were meant to be. We lean into the knowing, the intuition of who we be versus the ego-driven stay-safe-at-all-costs way of being.

The work of transformation will change your life. Courage is a requirement on this road. However, there are others who are further along the road who will lend a hand and hold yours as you walk along the rocky parts. Your work is your work. Much support is available to you in the way of coaches, therapists and friends who are walking the path to reclamation of who they be. Yes, there is help here, and ultimately, it is you who must choose the inner path. You were created with some gift, some talent - perhaps many gifts and many talents. The world needs the benefit of those gifts. We can be of service or not. Whatever we choose, it's all okay.

DAWN

Nature glows
With ecstasy
Sun peeks
Over the edge
Of the earth
Forest overflows
With light
And Love
Saturates
Green
Dew glistens
Reflecting the sacred
Within
My heart
Wide open
Beats to
The rhythm
Of life

You were created to express your gifts. We all were created with gifts that help heal the world. We need each other. You are important. Know that.

Inspired by Lao Tzu – Tao Te Ching – Chapter 64. "The journey of a thousand miles begins with one step."

ONE STEP

One step
Two step
The dance
Of life
Forward
Back
Lean in
Lean out
Moving
Toward
The
Unknown
Always
With
Love
Beside
Us

Darlene Versak 11/17/20

∞

The Power of One Step

In my first telephone conversation with my friend and life coach Jen Halterman, she asked me to do something. I was to note each time that I was defensive within the next week. Write it down and identify it. She told me that the "why" of doing the exercise was to determine how open I was to feedback. If I was going to coach someone, I would need to be open to feedback and not get defensive. I would need to take in what someone was saying - not in judgment, but with an ear for truth. Feedback is a giving and receiving kind of thing. I desired to be open to the process. I wanted to invite the Divine into each relationship. Coaching requires me to give feedback and to receive feedback. How open was I to considering other people's words and applying discernment versus judgment?

So, if a circumstance happened and I became defensive, I was to note that and what defense mechanism I chose to deal with it. For instance, if someone said something I deemed to be untrue about me, I might use denial as my coping mechanism. If something happened that I didn't like, I'd use distraction to move the conversation to something different. I was to note every time I got defensive. Using "yeah, but" in a sentence is a good indication of defensiveness. It's funny when someone who is trying to help you tells you something that A) you already think you are not (in this instance defensive), and B) you are unaware of. In this case, it was how many times I jump into defensive mode. My ego freaked out and did not want to comply. Truth is, I did the assignment for a day, then picked it up a few days later and fudged my results. So basically, I lied to myself.

Five minutes before we were to meet on our Zoom call, I could not find my paper with the tally of my results. I showed up, because that's what I do, and I asked her to please give me a few minutes to find the paper. Seriously, in hindsight, my ego was tossing its cookies at someone "seeing" through me. Anyhow, I found it and we began to go over how many times, in the normal course of a day, I was defensive. My ego's defense was, "Well you didn't really do the exercise; you made it up. It's not that bad." However, as we went over each defense mechanism (because remember, I was doing it the first day), I realized how much I defend the way that I think. The words, denial, anger, spiraling, nostalgia, anxiety, confusion, special, busyness, there was humor (yay for that) and resistance all seemed to hang over my head. At the time, I felt harsh judgment from her (I was projecting my judgment of myself onto her). I felt defeated, and the weight of myself fell on me. I felt shame. I felt guilt. By the way, none of those feelings are from love. This condemnation of myself was me beating myself up. I learned that this was my ego trying to keep me in place.

She urged me to watch the recording of our call. She told me to watch for signs of my ego showing up. What does my ego look like on the outside? Did I have any tells, like in poker? Could I see when my ego was reacting? Yuck, I thought. Why would I listen to her beat me up again? Yet, I knew somewhere within that she loved me, she cared about me and she was trying to help me. Of course, I ran away for a few weeks. My process has been to lean in, then lean out. I'll lean in a little until the fear comes up, and then lean out. Next time I'll lean in a little more, then lean out. Each of us is different. Your process might look nothing like mine.

When I finally did go back a few weeks later and watched myself, I saw the truth of it. My ego was in charge, not my true self.

She was so kind. She was not judging me. She held me with love. She spoke to me in kindness. She told me something that resonated in my core: that I can change one degree at a time. I can change one step at a time. If I become aware that I am doing it, I can change it. Instead of my ego controlling me, I could take my power back through choice. At the time, it felt like a cesspool of shit thinking. One step - that sounded doable. Tackling all of it at once, yeah, that wasn't going to work. But, one aspect of me? I could work on that. I could seek awareness and ask God for help in seeing how I use denial as a defense mechanism to hide the truth. Jen has a saying: "Universe, please show me what I'm unaware of." I added to that: "Universe, please show me in kindness what I'm unaware of." Because the Universe speaks in whispers, nudges and breadcrumbs. Sometimes I would miss them, and when you don't get the message in gentleness, sometimes you might get walloped over the head with truth. Hence, asking to be shown in kindness seemed like a good spell to cast.

I want truth to live and breathe through me.

www.youtube.com/watch?v=DUn6kYSnt3E
"Soulshine" – Govt Mule

CLOUDS

The clouds moved in
Silently on the breeze
Slowly they crept
Across the sky

I saw them coming
On the Horizon
They seemed to be far
But that was an illusion

I'd turned away
To do my work
Of opening my heart
To Love

Behind the clouds
And harsh words spoken
The Light shines
Waiting to melt away the pain
All shall be well

D. Versak 9-14-20

www.youtube.com/watch?v=hS-Y8dYD-Bg
(150) Beautiful Chorus - Inner Peace - YouTube
"Inner Peace" – Beautiful Chorus

The Call

A call rings in the stillness. You feel it when you're in the present moment. You may feel it in the dark night, in the gaze of a loved one or on a beautiful walk in nature. It is the call to Love. It's a magnetic pull of who and what we truly are - a vibration of energy that tugs at our heart and whispers to our soul. Remember who you are. Remember from whence you came. There's a homing device implanted in us by God so that when we tune into its frequency, we know the truth of it. We desire the alignment of energy - peace that surpasses all understanding. Peace.

The call asks us to look within. We are asked to strip away the layers of who we think we are. The labels, the titles, and the meanings we've learned and examine all of it through the lens of love. Judgment has no place here. Surrender, trust, and allowance seep into the shell of what we created. The barricades that had been erected to protect us are dismantled. The illusion dissolves. Most of us lean in and lean out of the process. If we choose to continue, what we find on the other side of the work is our authentic, wild, innocent heart that beats to the rhythm of life. The heart that connects to Source and each other. The heart intuitively knows we are all connected. We take the journey home as we choose.

There are no requirements. You need do nothing. You can choose to examine your life. You could seek to remove all obstacles to Love. You can choose to live in your heart space instead of in your head space (ego) or not. Always, it's your choice.

I started this year by attending an event called Expand 2020 hosted by Varian Brandon, a life coach I follow on Facebook. I found her through another life coach I worked with named Allison Crow, who was excellent in her ability to help women set up their businesses and remain authentic in the process. Life coaches are people who help you see your blind spots. They listen to your words and your stories and then sift for truth. They help you find a different perspective. They help you see circumstances from new perspectives. Most of all, they are truth tellers.

At Expand 2020 I had some revelations. Thirty women gathered to share their awareness with each other. What struck me was no one was in judgment of the other. Each of us shared our vulnerability in safety. No one talked about anyone else. We were present. We were witnesses. We were all there to expand our consciousness. Each attendee was at a different place in their journey. Some of us were just beginning and some were very accomplished women. No one was tearing anyone down. It was about speaking your truth and allowing others to see your heart. We felt each other. Having another human hear you helps you to identify (either by yourself or through what they see) areas that require more love. We found parts of ourselves that were ready for light and allowed love to enter and cleanse away the debris. We were doing the work of uncovering our blind spots and applying love to them so we could release that energy. Let it go. It was about unearthing the programming and stories that held us down and limited us. Being in the company of women who were walking the walk, talking the talk and living their truth in their lives was inspiring. The whole experience was uplifting for my soul.

The call goes out to each of us: be who you were created to be. Forgive. Be kind. Give and receive. Live in allowance of others. Dream. Create a life you love.

Gratitude Festival 7-14-17

Https://www.youtube.com/watch?v=4lx86B6a3kc

"Woodstock" - Crosby, Stills Nash & Young

TUMBLING WORDS

Before a word tumbles
Carelessly
Over my tongue
Out my lips
I pause

Are they chosen
These words
Particles of power
Enthused with
What energy

Is it my intention
Am I speaking
From Love
Or fear
Am I
In a space of alignment
Words flowing
Love dancing
In the spaces between
Waves of connection
Rolling between us

Or are my words born
Of chaos
Fear of loss swirling
Abandonment circles
Unworthy the spiral

It is my choice
Always

D. Versak 11/30/20

What We Focus On Grows

There once was a piece of white paper, and on that paper was a small black dot about a ½ inch in diameter in the bottom right corner an inch from the border. When students came into the classroom, they were asked to look at the paper and tell the teacher what they saw. Overwhelmingly, the answer was a black dot. It seemed that the large expanse of white paper had been subjugated to the background, and that one thing popped on that background. It stood out. It's like that in our lives. What we focus on matters. If we focus on what we have and all the things that are "right" in our lives, they grow and more goodness comes into our lives. We're looking for it. We're expecting it. We are bringing it into being. We've decided what we want our lives to look, touch, taste and feel like.

When we focus on the things that are "wrong" in our lives that grows too. The flat tire, the broken heater, the sickness lurking in the corner of our mind. Our thoughts matter. Learning to witness and examine them helps you unlock your personal power to choose. You can choose what you will focus on. You get to decide where your time, talent and energy will go. This is your great power. Most of us hardly think about how we think. That is like the line in the movie The Usual Suspects when Kevin Spacey says the greatest trick the devil ever pulled was convincing the world he didn't exist. We have forgotten the power in our words. There is power in our thoughts. We have forgotten the power of our story. The one we tell ourselves every day. The one that locks us into a script that was handed to us by our culture and families. If you feel dissonance in your life, perhaps this is the place it's coming from. The definition of dissonance according to Google Dictionary is, "The lack of harmony among musical notes." When the life you're living doesn't feel like your own. It is in this disconnection to self that we can begin to feel our way into waking up and consciously choosing to live as we were created to live.

This is where alignment and authenticity arrive on the scene. Somewhere we lose ourselves and then we feel the dissonance, the separation of who we are from who we desire and were created to be. In this life journey I felt the dissonance for a while before I did anything about it. Mostly, I denied it. I projected my stuff onto others and I distracted myself with the busyness of life. On the surface, I had forgotten the power of my words and I came to a place where I wasn't sure who I was anymore. The comfortable, familiar version of me was constricting and small. I knew how people wanted me to behave; and I couldn't plaster the smile on my face one more day and behave according to their desires.

Now, here's the thing: I am a happy person by nature. I've been called Polly Sunshine, June Cleaver, etc. So, for me to not be able to access my joy? That was devastating. We are given tiny nudges, gentle guidance from the Universe however, when we ignore the signs, the messages get louder as they try to get our attention. For me, it took a bullhorn from Spirit to get my attention. WAKE UP!!! We all came here to experience the contrast that exists on this planet. We came to create. Most of all, we came here to love in all of life's glorious variations – family, friends, lovers…all of it.

What you focus on grows, which is why gratitude journals are all the rage. Writing down three things a day that you are thankful for shifts your attention to celebrating what you have instead of focusing on what you lack. It's a shift in energy that attracts more good things into your life. When you can appreciate what you have and call it out, you then have the opportunity to attract more things to be grateful for. It doesn't have to be grand. It can be as simple as drinking a glass of water and being thankful that, to get water, all you have to do is turn on the tap.

All We Have is Now

I've hit some of the highlights and lowlights of my life in words, pictures, songs and poems. The shorthand version (for those old enough to remember when shorthand writing was a thing) goes as follows: child of an alcoholic, married with a carefully crafted picture-perfect family, cancer, divorce, transformation, writer, hiker and bad-ass friend. This is my story, my labels, and yet the words can never capture the essence of who I am.

The past is done. We go back to walk through it and glean nuggets of wisdom and we keep walking. We unstick ourselves from it by experiencing it, feeling all of it, forgiving it, forgiving others, forgiving ourselves, remembering the lessons and letting it go. Let it go! The sting has gone out of the bite. Yes, whatever trauma you've walked through lives in your body. However, when we do the work around it, we are able to release it and forgive that version of ourselves. We become free. It (the story, the past) is no longer in control. We are no longer hiding from it, burying it, doing our best to forget it. Shame and blame are not of the Spirit, so by releasing the shame and/or blame surrounding the story, we begin to live at choice and possibility. It's there, but it's not running the show. Our essence moves from the mind/ego (which is here for our protection but freaks out at a lot of things and was never meant to be in charge) to our heart (it's who we came here to be). Breath brings us to the present, which is all we have. When I pause instead of react, I take back my power. Breath centers us and brings us to the present moment.

What will I create in this moment?

What is possible?

I am Not A Victim. I am A Creator.

For much of my life, I held a victim's perspective. External circumstances happened and they determined what my reality would look like. I felt like a boat tossed about the ocean. A flat tire became that day's story. A fight with a friend became the drama du jour. Life was happening to me, and I felt like there was not much I could say or do to change things.

When I got divorced, I set off on the journey of transformation. At the time, I wouldn't have called it that. I would have called it doing things differently. I decided for my 50th year of life to try 50 new things. I had read, "I Dare Me" by TV journalist Lu Ann Cahn, in which she was challenged by her daughter to do something new (new meaning she hadn't done it in 10 years), every day and to show up on social media and talk/write about it. Lu Ann's adventure began with the polar plunge on January 1st (where you run into the ocean in freezing temperatures, which, in effect, "wakes" you up). Three hundred sixty-five days of newness seemed like a lot, so I decided for me, 50 would be a good number to commit to since I was turning 50.

I knew I wanted to practice courage. I knew I wanted to challenge myself in ways that I hadn't before. I wanted to feel alive in all my senses. I didn't want to get to the end of this journey and not have lived MY life. In Leo Tolstoy's book, "The Death of Ivan Llyich," the main character has behaved and done all of the things that society told him to do. He conformed to what was an acceptable life. In his dying, he asks himself the question: "What if I was wrong?" See, he never listened to his heart or the quiet messages of good that rose up within him. They were all suppressed, never allowed to be contemplated. He lived, but never truly lived.

Benjamin Franklin is quoted as saying, "Many people die at 25 and aren't buried until 75." I did not want that to be me. I lived that way up until I was 49, and I decided that it was time for me to get to know myself and truly live. I started following the breadcrumbs of soul. A friend asked me to go with her to a book signing event for "I Dare Me." I read the book and decided to institute my own version of 50 new things. In the midst of the 50 new things, I found a writing course called "Write Yourself Alive" by Andrea Bait. It attracted me, and I found enthusiasm in writing. I would not have called myself a writer before that. The course ended up changing my life. I met more people, took more courses, and I followed several breadcrumbs and nudges from Soul. And my life has been better for it. I had pieces published in Rebel Society, The Tattooed Buddha and Elephant Journal. I joined with a group of writers who also participated in "Write Yourself Alive" to put together a book called "Breathing Words," which showcased five of our writing pieces. In 2017, I became a published author.

What I also found along the way were people who helped me do my own work. Life coaches, mentors, books ("A Course in Miracles," "The Way of Mastery," "Gene Keys"), all of which pointed me in the direction of self-reflection. I directed my focus inward. Looking at the stories of my life, observing my ego at work, and seeing how the words I'd used, the words I'd been taught, the program that was downloaded from childhood to adulthood, had shaped the person that I had become.

Slowly, I began to unravel the stories. I pulled the threads of karma, picking delicately and, at times forcefully, to get to what it is that I truly desire. I began to create my life with intention. Examining my thoughts and feeling my feelings led me in choosing what direction to take next. My ego was no longer in charge. My energy shifted from my head to my heart. The ego is still here and the work of awareness is lifelong. The difference is now, there is less being triggered, and more peace in my life.

I took my power back. The power that was granted me as a child of God, Love, the Universe - whatever you want to call it. I am a powerful creator, and when I chose to breakup with the judgment of others and myself, I discovered freedom. You are a powerful creator, and when you choose to breakup with the judgment of others and yourself, you discover freedom. We are powerful creators, and when we choose to breakup with the judgment of others and ourselves, we discover freedom.

The journey from victimhood to freedom is a choice. It's a choice that we all have available to us. What is possible if we all choose freedom?

The trees whisper,
"Dragonfly, show me the art of becoming."

Resources

Here are two Guided Meditation's to move from fear to love. I play one of these when my brain is running on the hamster wheel. It has helped me fall asleep in stressful times.

https://www.youtube.com/watch?v=NEwRGJHkrQ0 - **Wayne Dyer Night Meditation – Listen for 21 nights to reprogram your subconscious**

https://www.youtube.com/watch?v=5T_QxR8aclQ 639 Hz - **PURE POSITIVE LOVE ENERGY Miracle Tone Healing Music | Heart Chakra Solfeggio Frequency**

Made in the USA
Monee, IL
20 June 2022

41cbc144-a3ce-48a5-a563-2fcb2fb51589R01